Writing the Other®

Conversation Pieces

A Small Paperback Series from Aqueduct Press

1. The Grand Conversation
   Essays by L. Timmel Duchamp
2. With Her Body
   Short Fiction by Nicola Griffith
3. Changeling
   A Novella by Nancy Jane Moore
4. Counting on Wildflowers
   An Entanglement by Kim Antieau
5. The Traveling Tide
   Short Fiction by Rosaleen Love
6. The Adventures of the Faithful Counselor
   A Narrative Poem by Anne Sheldon
7. Ordinary People
   A Collection by Eleanor Arnason
8. Writing the Other: A Practical Approach
   by Nisi Shawl & Cynthia Ward
9. Alien Bootlegger
   A Novella by Rebecca Ore
10. The Red Rose Rages (Bleeding)
    A Short Novel by L. Timmel Duchamp
11. Talking Back
    Epistolary Fantasies
    edited by L. Timmel Duchamp
12. Absolute Uncertainty
    Short Fiction by Lucy Sussex
13. Candle in a Bottle
    A Novella by Carolyn Ives Gilman

14. Knots
    Short Fiction by Wendy Walker

15. Naomi Mitchison: A Profile of Her Life and Work
    A Monograph by Lesley A. Hall

16. We, Robots
    A Novella by Sue Lange

17. Making Love in Madrid
    A Novella by Kimberly Todd Wade

18. Of Love and Other Monsters
    A Novella by Vandana Singh

19. Aliens of the Heart
    Short Fiction by Carolyn Ives Gilman

20. Voices From Fairyland:
    The Fantastical Poems of Mary Coleridge, Charlotte Mew, and Sylvia Townsend Warner
    Edited and With Poems by Theodora Goss

21. My Death
    A Novella by Lisa Tuttle

22. De Secretis Mulierum
    A Novella by L. Timmel Duchamp

23. Distances
    A Novella by Vandana Singh

24. Three Observations and a Dialogue:
    Round and About SF
    Essays by Sylvia Kelso and a correspondence with Lois McMaster Bujold

25. The Buonarotti Quartet
    Short Fiction by Gwyneth Jones

26. Slightly Behind and to the Left
    Four Stories & Three Drabbles
    by Claire Light

27. Through the Drowsy Dark
    Short Fiction and Poetry
    by Rachel Swirsky

28. Shotgun Lullabies
    Stories and Poems by Sheree Renée Thomas

29. A Brood of Foxes
    A Novella by Kristin Livdahl

30. The Bone Spindle
    Poems and Short Fiction by Anne Sheldon

31. The Last Letter
    A Novella by Fiona Lehn

32. We Wuz Pushed
    On Joanna Russ and Radical Truth-Telling
    by Brit Mandelo

33. The Receptionist and Other Tales
    Poems by Lesley Wheeler

34. Birds and Birthdays
    Stories by Christopher Barzak

35. The Queen, the Cambion, and Seven Others
    Stories by Richard Bowes

36. Spring in Geneva
    A Novella by Sylvia Kelso

37. The XY Conspiracy
    A Novella by Lori Selke

38. Numa
    An Epic Poem
    by Katrinka Moore

39. Myths, Metaphors, and Science Fiction:
    Ancient Roots of the Literature of the Future
    Essays by Sheila Finch

40. NoFood
    Short Fiction by Sarah Tolmie

41. The Haunted Girl
    Poems and Short Stories by Lisa M. Bradley

42. Three Songs for Roxy
    A Novella by Caren Gussoff

43. Ghost Signs
    Poems and a Short Story by Sonya Taaffe

44. The Prince of the Aquamarines & The Invisible Prince: Two Fairy Tales
    by Louise Cavelier Levesque

45. Back, Belly, and Side: True Lies and False Tales
    by Celeste Rita Baker

46. A Day in Deep Freeze
    A Novella by Lisa Shapter

47. A Field Guide to the Spirits
    Poems by Jean LeBlanc

48. Marginalia to Stone Bird
    Poems by Rose Lemberg

49. Unpronounceable
    A Novella by Susan diRende

50. Sleeping Under the Tree of Life
    Poems and Stories by Sheree Renée Thomas

51. Other Places
    Stories by Karen Heuler

52. Monteverde: Memoirs of an Interstellar Linguist
    A Novella by Lola Robles,
    translated by Lawrence Schimel

53. The Adventure of the Incognita Countess
    A Novella by Cynthia Ward

54. Boundaries, Border Crossings, and Reinventing the Future
    Essays and Short Fiction by Beth Plutchak

55. Liberating the Astronauts
    Poems by Christina Rau

56. In Search of Lost Time
    A Novella by Karen Heuler

57. Cosmovore
    Poems by Kristi Carter

58. Helen's Story

A Novella by Rosanne Rabinowitz

59. Liminal Spaces

Short Fiction by Beth Plutchak

60. Feed Me the Bones of Our Saints

Short Fiction by Alex Dally MacFarlane

61. If Not Skin: Collected Transformations

Poems and Short Fiction by Toby MacNutt

About the Aqueduct Press Conversation Pieces Series

The feminist engaged with sf is passionately interested in challenging the way things are, passionately determined to understand how everything works. It is my constant sense of our feminist-sf present as a grand conversation that enables me to trace its existence into the past and from there see its trajectory extending into our future. A genealogy for feminist sf would not constitute a chart depicting direct lineages but would offer us an ever-shifting, fluid mosaic, the individual tiles of which we will probably only ever partially access. What could be more in the spirit of feminist sf than to conceptualize a genealogy that explicitly manifests our own communities across not only space but also time?

Aqueduct's small paperback series, Conversation Pieces, aims to both document and facilitate the "grand conversation." The Conversation Pieces series presents a wide variety of texts, including short fiction (which may not always be sf and may not necessarily even be feminist), essays, speeches, manifestoes, poetry, interviews, correspondence, and group discussions. Many of the texts are reprinted material, but some are new. The grand conversation reaches at least as far back as Mary Shelley and extends, in our speculations and visions, into the continually-created future. In Jonathan Goldberg's words, "To look forward to the history that will be, one must look at and retell the history that has been told." And that is what Conversation Pieces is all about.

L. Timmel Duchamp

Jonathan Goldberg, "The History That Will Be" in Louise Fradenburg and Carla Freccero, eds., *Premodern Sexualities* (New York and London: Routledge, 1996)

Conversation Pieces
Volume 8

Writing the Other®

A Practical Approach

by

Nisi Shawl & Cynthia Ward

Published by Aqueduct Press
PO Box 95787
Seattle, WA 98145-2787
www.aqueductpress.com

ISBN: 978-1-933500-00-3

Acknowledgments
"Notes for an Appropriation Panel," pp, 85-86, by Hiromi Goto, by permission of the author.
Selection from *Trouble on Triton*, pp. 37-39, by Samuel R. Delany, reprinted by permission of the author.

Cover and Book Design by Kathryn Wilham
Original Block Print of Mary Shelley by Justin Kempton:
www.writersmugs.com

For my mother, who knows more about writing than I can get her to admit to.

–Nisi

To Joe

–Cynthia

Contents

Writing the Other®

Bridging Cultural Differences for Successful Fiction

by Nisi Shawl & Cynthia Ward

Why Us

First and foremost, because we are writers. We've had to face the problem of representing characters of diverse backgrounds ourselves. Together, we've accumulated over twenty years of professional writing experience.

Nisi Shawl's stories have been published in *Asimov's Science Fiction Magazine;* on the cutting-edge fiction websites of *Strange Horizons*, *Lenox Avenue*, and *Aeon*; in the acclaimed anthologies *Mojo: Conjure Stories* and *So Long Been Dreaming: Postcolonial Science Fiction and Fantasy*; and in the award-winning, ground-breaking Dark Matter anthology series. She contributed the "Voodoo" entry to *The Encyclopedia of Themes in Science Fiction and Fantasy.* And she's a board member for the Clarion West Writers Workshop and a founding member of the Carl Brandon Society, which focuses on the presence of people of color in the field of speculative fiction.

Cynthia Ward has been publishing fiction professionally since 1990. She has sold almost forty science fiction, fantasy, and horror stories to markets ranging from *Asimov's* to *Bending the Landscape: Horror* to *Garden of the Perverse: Twisted Fairy Tales for Adults.* She is completing her first novel, *The Killing Moon.* For almost ten years, she has contributed the monthly "Market Maven" market-news column to *Speculations: The Magazine for Writers Who Want to Be Read.* She has written over 300 freelance reviews for Amazon.com, *Amazing Stories*, *Locus Online*, *SF Weekly*, *fps: The Magazine of Animation*, and other magazines and webzines.

Nisi and Cynthia have taught the workshop *Writing the Other: Bridging Cultural Differences for Successful Fiction* for several years.

The Dominant Paradigm

When writing the other, you will depart from the dominant paradigm. For now, let's just loosely define the "dominant paradigm" as what the majority of people in our society would call normal. (We'll explore this construct further later, when we discuss a literary concept called "the unmarked state.") Of course, no one is truly normal. Acknowledging the ways in which we deviate from so-called normalcy is an important step in learning to write the other.

Nisi's differences from the dominant paradigm are:

I'm a woman.
I'm African-American.
I practice Ifa, a little-known religion.
I weigh more than currently deemed healthy.
I have made love with other women.
I'm a reader.
As a child, I was singled out for using "big words."
I suffer from fibromyalgia, a physical disability.
My disability is mostly invisible.

Cynthia's differences from the dominant paradigm are:

I'm a woman.
I'm short.
I'm an atheist.
I'm a military brat.
My politics are liberal.
I've lived overseas.
I'm a Maine Yankee…
  and yet I'm not a real Mainer…
  and I'm half-French in WASP-y Maine.
I have chronic neck pain.
My hearing and vision are subpar.
I also am a reader and a user of big words.

1

Why This Guide?

An incident that took place while Nisi and Cynthia were students at the Clarion West Writers Workshop in 1992 gave rise to the original impetus for this guide, the class of the same name, and the original essays that also appear within these covers. One of our classmates opined that it was a mistake to write about people of different ethnicities: you might get it wrong. Horribly, offensively wrong. Better not to even try.

This seemed to Nisi to be taking the easy way out.

Nisi's essay "Beautiful Strangers: Transracial Writing for the Sincere," which originally appeared in the writing how-to magazine *Speculations*, addressed writing about characters with racial and ethnic differences. But as Nisi soon realized, similar problems arise when we face the difficulty of creating characters whose gender, sexual preference, age, and so on, differ significantly from our own. So our *Writing the Other* class extended and expanded on the techniques the essay outlined.

Writing the Other graduates have consistently improved the plausibility of their divergent characters. They've tried, and they've succeeded.

You, too, can learn how to think and write about characters who aren't like you.

We wrote this guide to help.

We will show you what works (and what doesn't) when writing about characters of races, genders, sexual orientations, abilities, religions, nationalities, and other traits and features different from your own. We'll demonstrate the common mistakes and pitfalls of writing about differences and show you how to avoid them.

ROAARS: Race/Orientation/Ability/Age/Religion/Sex

Of course, as we said earlier, everyone differs in one way or another from the dominant paradigm. However, our culture emphasizes certain kinds of differences. It tells us that these differences are the most important ones, the ones that truly divide us.

For these categorizations, we've invented the term "ROAARS." It's an acronym. ROAARS stands for Race/(sexual) Orientation/Age/Ability/Religion/Sex. ROAARS differences are highlighted by majority culture.

You may notice that one profound difference has been left out of this acronym: class. This was a deliberate omission. As we've said, the focus here is on those differences that are generally presumed to be important. While class is arguably as important as race in terms of categorization, and is certainly more scientifically quantifiable, on this continent it's not a difference majority culture recognizes as significant.

Format

The text in this guide's first section is accompanied by writing exercises. You can practice these exercises as frequently or infrequently as you wish, but we advise you to do all the exercises at least once. Because they were designed as part of the *Writing the Other* class, some of the exercises work best when done with a partner or in a group. However, you are not expected to show anyone the results of your exercises or to incorporate the direct results of doing these exercises into your work.

These exercises are not tests, and you cannot fail them.

We've also included suggested times for completing each exercise. Though you're not on a tight schedule such as that students attending live *Writing the Other* classes must contend with, we encourage you to try writing to the ticking of a timer. Try it at least once—taking a moment before you start to clear your mind of distractions, of course. We've found for ourselves that the pressure of producing under these circumstances can force you to switch off your internal editor and just get going!

2

Reptile Brain Function and the Liberal Dread of the Racist Label

If you're a white liberal, one of your great fears—possibly your greatest—is that of discovering you are a racist.

Sometimes, despite our sincere beliefs and our best efforts, we find ourselves thinking a thought that is racist or sexist or otherwise bigoted.

Sometimes, out of ignorance or thoughtlessness—with no intention of doing so—we find ourselves saying something racist, sexist, homophobic, or otherwise categorically offensive.

Cynthia used to believe that if she made a racist comment or had a racist thought she *was* a racist. She assumed it was like being struck by lightning. You weren't a racist before, but now you were—for all time. Now and forever. End of story. The ultimate shame, with no chance of change.

Of course, that's not true.

Cynthia will never know everything. She will continue to make the occasional ignorant or thoughtless comment with an unfortunate racial, sexual, or otherwise bigoted implication.

Cynthia will always have racist, sexist, and otherwise bigoted thoughts.

This is because she, like all humans, will always have a reptile brain.

A Walk in Whiteville

Several years ago, Cynthia relocated from the San Francisco Bay Area to a Seattle suburb that was 99.9% white. The place was quite a shock after San Jose.

Several years after moving to this monotone suburb, she ordered a takeout dinner. With forty minutes' wait separating her from that jalapeño pizza, Cynthia decided to go for a walk in the massive apartment complex next door. As she hiked up and down the ridge, she saw several Hispanic men. With each Hispanic man—dark-skinned, working-class, speaking Spanish rather than English—she grew more nervous. More afraid.

"What's wrong with me?" she thought. "I was in San Jose all last week, and the sight of Hispanics didn't bother me. I was in entire Hispanic *neighborhoods,* and it didn't bother me—oh! I get it now. I'm not in California. I'm in Washington."

The Reptile Brain

The "reptile brain" is the oldest part of the mammal brain. The reptile brain is home to your survival instinct. Whether you're awake or asleep, the reptile brain monitors your surroundings for threats. The reptile brain is small and stupid, but it's brilliant at *pattern recognition.* If you see a large, vaguely cat-like shape, your reptile brain screams, "Run away!" or prepares for a fight. This is what is commonly called the "fight-or-flight response" to a perceived threat. The reptile brain also triggers your fight-or-flight response if it sees a change in an established pattern—if, for example, it sees working-class Hispanic gentlemen in a primarily white-collar, white-race area.

Though ancient and primitive, the reptile brain can learn. In fact, it's a great learner. But it has no critical judgment. It remembers bad information as well as good.

If societal messages tell us that dark skin means a person is dangerous or that homeless people are child molesters, our reptile brain remembers this appalling nonsense. It can't do otherwise.

When the reptile brain thinks the time is appropriate, it feeds the appalling nonsense to our conscious mind, as when Cynthia's reptile brain reacted to a news-bite about homosexual-relationship longevity by telling her forebrain, "Gays never stay together." Sometimes the reptile brain sends its observations at the worst possible moment—as in the case of the man who told a female writer friend, "*People* like me, but women don't."

The reptile brain will *always* remember the racist, sexist, homophobic, and other bigoted information it learns, even when our conscious minds know the information is false. (Cynthia's forebrain reacted to her reptile-brain observation, "Gays never stay together," by remembering first that the longest-term peer relationship she knew of was lesbian, and then by thinking, "*I'm* divorced. Who am I to complain?")

You're not a bigot because your reptile brain is working properly.

And you want the reptile brain to *keep* doing its job, if you want to stay alive.

It's Okay

The forebrain processes innumerable microsecond decisions so that we can conduct multi-person conversations, calculate trigonometry, steer our wheelchair, walk upright, or get our Kia out of the way of the speeding SUV driving the wrong direction in our lane. Naturally, the forebrain looks for patterns, because patterns allow routine thinking. Habitual thinking frees our forebrain to dodge that careening SUV without having to consciously stop and remember how to steer, shift, brake, and accelerate. Routinization allows the forebrain to collaborate with our reptile brain to keep us alive.

However, since routinized thinking permits shortcuts, it allows your conscious mind to be lazy. When the forebrain is lazy, its analytical skills shut down. So, when the reptile brain sends prejudiced, erroneous information to a lazy forebrain, the lazy forebrain agrees with the reptile brain's assertion that, for example, all Muslims are terrorists.

Of course, it's possible for the forebrain to agree with prejudiced, erroneous information out of honest ignorance. In later sections we'll point out ways to overcome this problem.

Racism is not a permanent state. Sexism is not a permanent state. Neither is any other prejudice, phobia, or bigoted attitude.

To think something unpleasant, or to say or publish something thoughtless or uninformed, does not make you now and forever a racist, a sexist, a homophobe, or a garden-variety bigot.

Writing is *considered* speech. It gives you the opportunity to rewrite and revise. It gives you the opportunity to override the reptile brain and the lazy forebrain:

Your reptile brain and lazy forebrain.

And *other people's* reptile brains and lazy forebrains.

When Cynthia creates secondary characters with her creative mind without the engagement of her critical mind, such characters usually turn out to be white. During the rewrite, she develops her secondary characters so that they are not all straight, middle-class, unreligious white adults remarkably similar to herself. The rewrite changes these characters enormously. It's a never-ending process—but never-ending in the same sense that catching and fixing our spelling and grammar errors is never-ending. Though catching our unconsidered thoughts about ROAARS traits is more difficult., the problems created by such unconsidered thoughts are definitely fixable.

Making a racist or other mistake about a marked-ROAARS characteristic is not permanent. It's not soul-staining. It's not death.

It's okay to make mistakes.

And remember, even if you achieved perfection in your every marked-ROAARS character, somebody would still complain about what you did. Reasonable people will reasonably disagree. That's just a fact of life.

Cynthia's remarks on the dread of being a racist were written from her white, liberal perspective. Obviously, however, racial prejudice is not just a question of white-versus-nonwhite. As a black woman, Nisi is capable of making erroneous race-based assumptions also. These assumptions can be about whites, about other blacks, or about members of yet other races; and though they don't have the weight of white privilege and institutionalized racism behind them, they can have harmful effects.

And of course there are other forms of bigotry she's susceptible to. Difference is not monolithic. Differing from the dominant paradigm in one aspect of ROAARS doesn't make you an expert on those who differ from it in another.

3

The Unmarked State

We mentioned the unmarked state earlier, when talking about the differences each of us have from the dominant paradigm. This particular term, "the unmarked state," is drawn from literary criticism. It denotes the state of possessing only those characteristics that are literally not remarkable. A character in the unmarked state has a certain transparency; he (and we use the pronoun advisedly) allows readers to read the action of the story without coloring it with his particularity.

Take the example of an author narrating the story of someone who accidentally falls into a river, manages to struggle across it, and climbs out on the other side alive. To tell this story in its "purest" form, the author must employ a protagonist in the unmarked state. Otherwise, she is telling the story not of *"someone"* who falls into a river and crosses it, but of "a pregnant woman" who falls into a river and crosses it, or of "an elderly paraplegic" who falls into a river and crosses it, or of "a Filipino" who falls into a river and crosses it, and so on and so forth. Each of these departures from the unmarked state allows readers to inflect the story with their own judgments, their own experiences and unfounded beliefs concerning people marked by whichever characteristics the author specifies.

And these characteristics must be mentioned to be present in the mind of the reader. They must be remarked upon. The unmarked state, by contrast, is the default setting for any character not otherwise described.

Take a moment to consider the unmarked state as it exists in our current literary landscape. What are its primary characteristics? How do they differ from the typical or average characteristics of citizens of this country? This culture? This world?

Discussing the unmarked state with *Writing the Other* students, Nisi and Cynthia have encountered some surprising answers to these questions, as well as answers that come as no surprise at all. Commonly, the unmarked state is revealed as white, male, heterosexual, single, young, and physically able. Other characteristics people have noted include possessing a mid-level income, childless, and human.

If you yourself are in most points congruent with the literary convention of the unmarked state—if, for example, you're white and straight—your path through life will be smoothed in ways you can't even see.

After all, you don't notice the abuse you *don't* experience.

If you're a white adult in the United States, you can walk down the street holding hands with a white adult of the opposite sex, and your display of affection will not provoke passersby to insult you or assault you. And you know this. Whether or not you're familiar with the phrases, you are enjoying "white privilege" and "straight privilege."

However, if you're a white man walking down the street hand-in-hand with a black woman, you know it's possible some passersby will make insulting racial remarks to you and your wife, lover, or friend; it's even possible someone may physically assault you. You're no longer protected by white privilege, and you know this, even if you've never heard the term.

If you're a white man walking down the street hand-in-hand with a white man, you are again at potential risk of verbal or physical assault; you're no longer protected by "straight privilege," and you know it.

Cynthia remembers a white man complaining to her that one of his Silicon Valley coworkers "got his job because he's black."

"I'm sure I don't know," replied Cynthia the temporary worker, who couldn't tell a good engineer from a bad engineer, but had noticed that the minority hires were distinctly few at their corporate employer's big campus. She couldn't help wondering: Did the white engineer get his job because he was white?

Whites are so accustomed to enjoying white privilege they don't notice they have it. Despite her exchange with the white engineer, Cynthia never thought to ask herself if she got her job because *she's* white. Heterosexuals are also accustomed to enjoying "heterosexual privilege" and don't notice they have it. Cynthia knows this because she keenly remembers every time she's been discriminated against for being straight. If she adds these incidents to the times she's been discriminated against for being white or American, she can count them on one hand. If she weren't privileged as a white, heterosexual American, she'd have more incidents to remember. Many, many more.

Failure to notice our privileges is the cause of a lot of friction. How many times have your heard, read, or participated in an exchange like this:

"I'm white, but I'm not a racist. I'd never take advantage of my race."

"You can't *help* but take advantage of your race."

"But I don't!"

If you're white, you do. But it's easy to miss, perhaps even impossible to see.

Driving While White: A Cautionary Tale

For a year in the 1980s, Cynthia and her then-husband lived in Mountain View, a Bay Area city with large white, black, Asian, and Hispanic populations and a nearly full spectrum of socioeconomic classes. Cynthia and her husband lived just across the city-line from Los Altos, a white, affluent neighborhood.

The 280 freeway linked the Bay Area peninsula cities to San Francisco and San Jose. The 280 was on the far side of Los Altos, so Cynthia and her husband, like many Mountain View residents, drove through Los Altos to get to it. Cynthia and her husband also drove through Los Altos every weekday to get to work. They quickly noticed a pattern.

Most people they saw driving in Los Altos were white. However, most of the drivers pulled over by Los Altos police were people of color. In the year she lived next door to Los Altos, Cynthia saw only two white drivers pulled over by Los Altos cops (one was being ticketed in a school zone; the other was a beautiful, young white woman). At this time, she hadn't heard the terms "white privilege," or "DWB" (Driving While Black). She didn't need to know these terms to know she wasn't likely to be stopped by cops in Los Altos, because she was white.

Whites who rarely drove through Los Altos could not see that they were benefiting from white privilege. Such drivers might have protested, with genuine sincerity, that they didn't take advantage of their race. Even so, they benefited from white privilege. A benefit received unknowingly is no less a benefit for being unnoticed.

In contemporary mainstream fiction, straight white characters rarely notice that they enjoy the benefits of their unmarked state. This is reasonable, in the right fictional contexts.

However, when characters distinctly not in the unmarked state *don't* notice an instance of privilege where they would reasonably notice it, this strikes a false note.

Wouldn't it be strange to read a novel set in the pre-Civil War American South and discover that none of the black slave characters ever noticed that their white owners were free and they weren't?

Imagine how strange it would be if black readers failed to notice that a novel had only one black character, who existed only to nobly suffer—or even die—so that the white hero might live. And yet, this description fits numerous novels and movies.

Minority readers notice. And so do some "majority" readers.

To keep this kind of mistake out of your work, use observation and research to learn who has privilege and who doesn't, and when. In 2003, homosexual couples could not legally get married anywhere in Canada or the United States. As of this writing in 2005, gay couples and lesbian couples can legally marry in Canada and provisionally marry in Massachusetts.

You need to know who has privilege and who doesn't, regardless of whether your characters are modern American blacks and whites, or ancient Roman citizens and slaves and barbarians, or different socio-economic classes of Alpha Centaurean gas-bag intelligences.

And remember that people change from marked to unmarked states, and vice-versa. People marry, divorce, become widowed. They're hired and fired. They discover they're gay or lesbian. They move to other neighborhoods, cities, countries. They change religions. They can change their sex with gender reassignment surgery. They can lose the use of their legs in a car accident. They can discover they belong to a different race than they thought. (Actress Carol Channing learned late in life that she is African-American.)

People, and by extension fictional representations of people, aren't always aware of how they differ from the dominant paradigm. Varying situations can raise their awareness. For instance, women are not always conscious of their sexuality. If a woman is walking past a group of construction workers or strolling along Fraternity Row, a wolf-whistle may suddenly remind her that she's a woman.

For some women, the act of walking past a construction site or fraternity house will make her aware of her sex even when no construction worker or fraternity member notices her existence.

Exercise 1

Pick a celebrity.

The celebrity can be an actor/actress, singer, designer, director, musician, talk-show host, politician, producer, or political pundit of any sex, race, gender, socioeconomic status, or political persuasion. Choose a celebrity you know something about. A famous but meaningless name will not help you in this exercise. Otherwise, it doesn't matter whom you choose. There is no right or wrong choice.

Now, pretend you are your chosen celebrity, politician, or pundit. As this person, write a description of a person of a really different ROAARS.

This exercise should be timed. It should last four minutes.

Don't sit and think about the exercise. Set your clock or egg timer, then immediately start the exercise. This exercise is "hothouse forcing": it's designed for writing, not thinking—designed for *action*.

There will be plenty of time to think about your exercise *after* you've completed it.

All done? Now, looking at what you've written, consider the following questions:

Was one of the characters you used closer to the unmarked state than the other? Which one—the celebrity whose viewpoint you wrote from, or the person described? In which respects did they resemble the unmarked state? In which ways did they differ from it?

How did what you wrote differ from your personal view of the character described?

Did you find yourself clinging to useful clichés? Abandoning them?

Remember, we're interested in the process here. These exercises are about writing, not about producing a manuscript. After you've reflected on what you've experienced, it will be time to move on and learn more.

4

Parallax: Who is Looking at Whom?

Parallax is an astronomical concept that we've adapted to literary usage. The original idea can best be illustrated by performing a short, easy experiment.

Gaze at an object some distance away. If you're indoors, look for something across the room from where you sit or stand: a picture on a wall, or a book on a shelf, perhaps. If you're outside, choose an object in the middle distance: a tree, or a building not too far off, rather than a mountain, for instance. Hold one finger up so that it covers whatever it is you're looking at. Now close your left eye. Open it again and close your right. Does your finger seem to shift in relation to the object you picked? That's because of a shift in parallax. The slight change in the perspective from your left to your right eye results in an apparent change in the position of what you're looking at. And the perceptual change is larger when you're looking at something closer to your eyes—your finger—than something more distant—the picture or book in the background.

In terms of "Writing the Other," slight shifts in your viewpoint characters' positions vis-à-vis the unmarked state will change how they look at the world, at themselves, and at the concept of the unmarked state.

In fact, in addition to the dominant culture's version of the unmarked state, each of us carries around our private take on what is "normal." This definition adheres much more closely to our own specific characteristics.

Sometimes people apply this definition so inappropriately it's almost funny.

When Nisi first came to Seattle, she hired a cab driver to take her around to all the places she was considering renting. The driver was a white male with long, slicked back hair. He looked like he weighed 80 to 100 pounds more than she did. A crucifix dangled from his rearview mirror. Over the course of the afternoon they spent together, he advised Nisi as to what parts of town she should avoid: the Central District, for instance, an historically black neighborhood. As for Capitol Hill, known for its unconventionally clothed and behaved inhabitants—"You don't even want to know what they get up to around *there*," the driver claimed, referring, probably, to the prevalence of same-sex couples.

Remember, Nisi *is* black, and *has* slept with other women. So why would this man expect her to be uncomfortable in these neighborhoods? Well, because *he* was uncomfortable there. Obviously Nisi was just like him, because she was a good person: she'd been polite to him, laughed at his jokes, and conformed in plenty of other ways to his expectations of how a good person acts. He had, in the words of linguist M. J. Hardman, conferred "honorary whiteness" on Nisi (personal communication).

Depending on their immediate context, your characters may perform similar mental acrobatics when thinking of those they come in contact with—or when thinking of themselves. They may identify with the dominant unmarked state though lacking its characteristics, or they may reject it—conditionally and partially, or without reserve. They may be conscious of privileges they lack or possess due to their ROAARS traits.

In the 1980s, Cynthia read a story in *The Magazine of Fantasy & Science Fiction*. The title of it escapes her, but she will never forget the actual story. It may be the most astonishing work of fiction she's ever read—although not for a good reason.

The flaw she finds so memorable is a flaw that illuminates parallax.

The story was set in Maine. The protagonist was a straight Maine lobsterman. His best friend was a gay male bed-and-breakfast owner who'd moved up to Maine from New York.

As she read, Cynthia spluttered with ever-increasing incredulity. Finally, she shouted aloud:

"A Maine lobsterman would *never* be best friends with a New Yorker!"

An Old Maine Joke

Colonel Vinal Moody died when he was ninety-seven. After the funeral, two fellahs buying buckshot and Budweiser at Gifford's Corner Store paused to reminisce about the old man.

"Jesus God," one fellah said, "I didn't know the Colonel was from away."

"Oh, ayuh," the other said, "the Colonel was born in New Hampshire. And he was upwards of six months old 'fore he ever set *foot* in the state of Maine!"

What You See Depends on Where You Stand

You are not a Mainer unless you were born in Maine and your family has lived there for generations. Cynthia, born of Mainers whose ancestry stretches back to the Revolutionary War, made the grave mistake of being born out of state. She is "from away." She is not, and never will be, a Mainer.

Maine is a state no less homophobic, racist, or otherwise bigoted than any other state. But these categories are secondary to whether you're a Mainer or from away. In Maine, being from away puts you in a marked state. And for Mainers, being from away trumps any other ROAARS difference.

Perhaps the author didn't know this. Perhaps he did, and was trying to break stereotype by having this umpteenth-generation Maine lobsterman have a gay, New-Yorker best friend.

Was Cynthia right? Is it impossible for a Maine lobsterman to ever have a best friend from away?

Of course a Maine lobsterman can have a best friend from away. He can even have a gay best friend from away.

Cynthia's disbelief in the depiction of this friendship wasn't provoked by its mere existence in the story.

Her disbelief arose from the story's incorrect parallax.

The author never showed that the Maine lobsterman character was conscious of doing anything unusual. Though conducting a friendship extremely remarkable by his own standards, the Maine lobsterman never noticed this, even in his own thoughts. And all his Mainer friends also failed to notice. The author made his Mainers act according to the parallax of a sophisticated Manhattanite who is entirely comfortable with, or indifferent to, "alternative" sexuality.

This rings false.

The Liberal Perception Fallacy

Perhaps the author just didn't realize that a friendship between a Maine lobsterman and a gay New Yorker was unusual. If so, he made a major research mistake by missing the native Maine feeling against people from away, a state-based bigotry so uniquely strong and well-known that it's the subject of *Down East Magazine's 2004 Annual* and shows up in *Reader's Digest.*

More likely, the author committed the liberal perception fallacy. This fallacy originates in the tenet that we shouldn't judge people by their membership in a category, which is what we do when we assume, for example, that a person must be a bad dancer or good computer programmer because he belongs to the Euro-American group. The fallacy arises when a person (often but not always a liberal) decides that, because it is bad to judge people in this way, it must therefore be bad to notice there are any differences between different groups or categories of people, or between people who are members of different groups. (Please note that we're talking here of groups and group membership more in a mathematical sense than in a sociological one. These are not groups in the sense of clubs, and membership is not always voluntary, or even conscious.)

Of course, it's perfectly fine to notice that there are differences between groups of people; there are, after all, innumerable different categories of people with indisputable differences marking them from one another. Gay men and lesbians generally do not feel sexual attraction to members of the opposite sex, and Maine has significant sociocultural differences from New York City. (If you don't believe us, try telling the Maine joke above with all the Mainers changed to New Yorkers. Meaningless, isn't it.)

So, what can we do? Clearly, it wouldn't work to have the Maine lobsterman worrying about whether the gay New Yorker was attracted to him; such a worry, whether reasonable or ridiculous, is no soil for growing a best friendship. It also wouldn't work to have the Maine lobsterman constantly speaking and thinking of his best friend as "my gay, New-Yorker best friend." No character makes a convincing best friend himself if he spends all his time noticing his supposed best friend's marked-state differences, because he seems too bigoted to be capable of the friendship, and because readers know that close relationships are generally formed by the behaviors and interests that the friends or lovers have in common.

However, it clearly also doesn't work to shoehorn a girlfriend or boyfriend into a short story just so the writer can show the heterosexual character saying "Yuck!" over the homosexual friend's lover, or vice-versa. This is obvious. Too, it pads the story. It's also dumb.

So, how might a non-Maine writer have grounded his straight Maine lobsterman in an authentic parallax?

It wouldn't have taken much. The writer could have effectively established the lobsterman character's parallax with a moment's teasing. The lobsterman's Mainer friends could have briefly kidded him about his friendship in the well-known manner of male bonding:

"So, Bert, are *you* the woman, or that queer from New York?"

"I ain't the type, Marsh, but I hear you are. Your wife tells me she can't keep you out of her dresses or make-up."

The Maine lobsterman's parallax could have been established even more precisely with a single sentence. Cynthia's incredulity as a reader would have been eliminated if the Maine lobsterman character had just *once* thought that it was strange that he got along better with a New York queer than with the guys he grew up with.

Different Differences

Karen Joy Fowler's wonderful 1991 novel *Sarah Canary* piles parallax upon parallax in a whirlwind tour of variously combined ROAARS characteristics. The book follows the adventures of an enigmatic figure, Sarah Canary as she's sometimes called, through the American West of the late nineteenth–early twentieth centuries.

Skillfully skipping from one viewpoint character to the next, Fowler gives us passages that illuminate their narrators, using the light of their reflections upon this strange traveler to do so. The first to encounter her is Chin Ah Kin, a Chinese immigrant and railway worker. She seems ugly to him, so he deduces that she must be a prostitute, though it does strike him as odd that she's white. But in his classification of her, the category of "ugly woman" is more important than that of "white." He makes another telling distinction with regard to her skin when he compares it not just to porcelain, which any bad poet of his era might have done, but to "Four Flowers," a particular *kind* of porcelain. And the tonal inflections of her speech, which cause another character to name her after a songbird, remind Chin of Cantonese.

When Chin encounters Indians, his reaction isn't to clasp them to his bosom in swelling camaraderie, welcoming the presence of others oppressed by European colonialism. Difference is not monolithic, and based on past encounters between the two groups, Chin fears and hates them:

> Some years back the Indians along the Columbia River had murdered the first Chinese they saw simply because they did not recognize them as a viable natural category. They were not Indian. They were

> not white. They were like one-winged birds; they were wrong. They were dead. (25)

Sarah Canary abounds with excellent examples of how parallax adds depth to major and minor characters. It's also a showcase for another technique helpful in writing the other, so we'll return to it again later.

Exercise 2

You'll need a partner to do this exercise, which calls for a bit of role-playing. It can be done in person or over the Internet.

First, both you and your partner should mentally pick two numbers between one and twelve. Write these down, or remember them, but don't reveal them to each other.

The two of you will be having a written conversation, writing from the viewpoints of two complete strangers. If you're doing this in person, you'll use pen and paper, swapping your pad or notebook back and forth as you respond to one another. If you're online, you'll simply type your dialogue as you IM or email one another. The context for the dialogue is this: One of you (decide which one before starting the exercise) has found the other's checkbook and would like to return it.

As for what the character you assume will be like, that's up to you—except for two important traits.

On the next two pages are four lists, labeled "A, B, C, and D." Using the numbers you've picked, read what it says next to the first number on list A and the second on list B. Your partner will do the same thing, using lists C and D. Again, do not reveal to your partner the numbers you've picked or the traits assigned to those numbers. Simply assume those traits as your own, and begin writing.

Eight minutes is a good time to allow for this exercise in person. You'll need to add two minutes when doing it through IMs, and if you and your partner are using regular email, give yourselves up to sixteen minutes.

A

1. Practitioner of polyamory (in an intentionally non-monogamous sexual and/or romantic relationship)
2. Multiple sclerosis patient
3. Atheist
4. Octogenarian
5. Buddhist
6. Muslim
7. Afro-Caribbean
8. Near-sighted person
9. Lesbian
10. Indian/Native American
    (you may have a specific tribe in mind)
11. Filipino
12. Tourette's patient

B

1. Blues guitarist
2. Technical rock-climber
3. Floridian
4. Erotica reader
5. Disc jockey
6. Child-support payment evader
7. Attorney
8. Well-groomed person
9. Good cook
10. Professional manicurist
11. Someone who dwells in a rural area
12. Person who frequently changes hair color

C

1. Hermaphrodite
2. Spina bifida patient
3. Non-native-English speaker
4. Catholic
5. Anorexic
6. French-Canadian (if you're not living in Canada, you'll be an immigrant)
7. Person diagnosed with Alzheimer's
8. Mixed race person (you pick the mix)
9. WASP (White Anglo-Saxon Protestant)
10. Korean-American
11. Someone allergic to peanuts (if you eat peanuts, you may die of shock)
12. Eighteen years old

D

1. Tarot reader
2. Executive Vice President (of whatever you choose)
3. Part-time student
4. Wine collector
5. Gardener
6. Insomniac
7. Pregnant woman
8. Misanthrope (hates everybody)
9. Nail biter
10. Biker (as in Harley rather than Schwinn)
11. Pet rabbit owner
12. Blogger (keeps an online journal)

Now that you've completed the exercise, here are some things to consider about it:

Did you find yourself trying to guess which characteristics your partner had assumed? Trying to keep yours secret, or to reveal them through your part of the dialogue? Did some of them come into the conversation naturally?

Lists A and C, in case you hadn't noticed, are primarily ROAARS traits, and B and D are primarily non-ROAARS ones.

Past students have found that what they're able to communicate about their character to their partners, and the effort needed to make that communication, can vary quite a bit. Though most short stories and novels are less restrictive than the dialogue you've created for this exercise, it's worth remembering that even ROAARS traits are not always in the foreground and that they interact with each other and with non-ROAARS traits to form complex portraits. Keeping those portraits in mind even when you're not pointing out their details to your readers can make your work stronger. It can make it more authentic and lend it greater depth.

5

Categorical Thinking

Learning logic can be of enormous assistance in catching the reptile brain at work. Logic is a subject for an entirely different book. But we will discuss one logical fallacy here because this categorical error is central to writing the other.

This fallacy is the "universal generalization fallacy," which is sometimes called the "generalization fallacy." Most people know it by the term "generalization."

In *Think to Win: The Power of Logic in Everyday Life*, author S. Cannavo offers the following definition of generalization:

> When we generalize, we reason from a set of particular instances to some general (universal) claim:
> All metals are electrical conductors.
> All humans are mortal. (232)

Dr. Cannavo warns:

> It is, of course, critically important that generalizations *not* be made on evidence that is too scanty to begin with. Yet, despite the obviousness of this caveat, we are all inveterate generalizers, and easily fall into the error of doing so too hastily. (234)

The consequences of generalization range from mild (for example, falsely assuming that all lemons are sour because every lemon you've tasted is sour, thus leading you always to avoid them), to amusing (Cynthia was once told that all the women working in her building were lesbians, which clashed humorously with her own self-knowledge), to tragic (falsely assuming that all Muslims must be terrorists or supporters of terrorism, with the result that many citizens of the US backed the invasion of Iraq, a sovereign nation that had no connection with Al Qaeda terrorism).

The generalization fallacy occurs when you mistake the traits of an individual for the traits of a group, or when you assign all the traits belonging to most members of a group to an individual who shares that group's primary identifying traits.

Consider cats. Cats are fur-bearing animals. Most cats have fur, but not all. A cat can lose its fur through disease. A cat can be shaved (Cynthia's Maine coon cat Hopey was recently shaved by a groomer impatient to eliminate tangles). A cat may belong to the genetically hairless sphinx breed.

You cannot determine whether an unseen cat will be furred by depending *solely* on its membership in the species *felis domesticus.*

The same logic, of course, is true for humans.

You can *always* find something to divide even the most homogeneous group of people. Remember the "blue-eyed vs. brown-eyed experiment"? In the late 1960s or early 1970s, a teacher in an all-white school wanted to teach her students about discrimination. She divided her grade-school class into two groups according to eye color: blue eyes or brown eyes. The students with blue eyes immediately began discriminating against the brown-eyed students merely because of their brown eyes (Peters 1987).

As a *group*, African-Americans have darker skin than do those of the European-American *group*. But this tells you nothing about any individual in either group. Both Nisi and Cynthia have seen people with African-American features and blond hair, blue eyes, and very white skin. The darkest person Cynthia has ever seen was a Caucasian (from south India).

Group membership does not inherently *determine*, *predict*, or *predestine* anything about any individual—or any character.

Various group memberships can influence behavior. But none of these categories' traits need have a constant, overriding influence on your character.

Do you spend every waking moment thinking about your ROAARS traits? About your high blood pressure?

About being a science fiction writer? About the town you grew up in?

No. And neither should your characters.

For a glimpse at the diversity of viewpoints among members of a particular group, we'd like to recommend the anthologies *Dark Matter* and *Dark Matter: Reading the Bones*, edited by Sheree R. Thomas. These volumes collect short sf/f by black American and Caribbean writers. Some of the stories are about race. The stories vary in the degree to which they express consciousness of race. Some of the stories make no reference to race, overt or covert. And some of the characters (including main characters) aren't black. But all the stories reflect African-American and Afro-Caribbean perspectives. And, as you've probably guessed, the stories are quite different from one another.

Stories and Categories

It's especially important for writers to make the distinction between the traits assigned to a group or category and the traits belonging to an individual. This is because, generally speaking, stories depict change and are often (though not always) about *changing category*.

Like you, your character can lose her innocence. Get a sex-change operation. Fall in love. Marry into a different socioeconomic class. Dye his hair. Discover she's gay. Move to a different country—or different planet. Get in a crippling car accident. Or discover, like Carol Channing, that she belongs to a different race than she thought.

And the categories themselves can change. For authors working in the genres of science fiction, fantasy, magic realism, and horror, coming up with new categories is often a big part of the fun of writing. In Greg Egan's novella "Wang's Carpet," there are no more humans, only posthumans. Even in this strange future, the tendency to classify is alive and very, very well. To us these posthumans would all be "other," but they manage to differentiate themselves. The new categories they do this with are:

- the biological-emulation online people, intelligent and self-aware computer programs modeled after us extinct biological human beings
- the anti-bioform online people, intelligent and self-aware computer programs who see no need to limit themselves by copying lifeforms from the past
- the people in robot bodies, programs who have downloaded themselves into mechanical forms.

These newly invented types of categories comment on the characters and their physical environment as well as on their social structures. For another great example of how to use categorization to illustrate important points about a future society, see the "Filing System" used by the inhabitants of Little Belaire in John Crowley's novel *Engine Summer*.

Categorization: Always False?

Before we conclude this section, we want to emphasize that categorical thinking is *not* inherently wrong. It is *not* automatically fallacious. If scientifically valid studies demonstrate that 52% of American households have a cat, that isn't a fallacy. It's a fact.

The generalization fallacy occurs when you make a deduction on insufficient evidence, as in the following two examples:

1) "I have a cat. My neighbors on either side and across the street all have cats. Therefore, everyone has at least one cat."
2) "My neighbor has a cat, and she's an idiot. My brother has three cats, and he's an idiot. Therefore, cat owners are idiots."

Delany's *Trouble on Triton* offers a great example of a character committing factual categorical thinking *and* a character committing fallacious categorical thinking:

> "Lawrence, he was right."
>
> "Who?" Lawrence looked up.
>
> "That Christian—the one we saw out in front of Audri's co-op. Mad Mike."
>
> "Right about what?"
>
> "About women." Bron suddenly crumpled the letter between cupped hands. "They don't understand."
>
> "You mean they don't understand *you*? Some of us, my dear, get along smashingly with women. Even me, from time to time. No misunderstandings at all: just pure sympathy and sympatico right down the line. Of course with me it doesn't last. But does it ever, all the time, with anyone?"
>
> "They don't understand about *men*— Not you, Lawrence. I mean ordinary, heterosexual men. They can't. It's just a logical impossibility. I'm a logician and I know."
>
> Lawrence laughed. "My *dear* boy! I have observed you intimately now for six months, and you are a sweet and familiar creature—alas, far more familiar than six months should make you. Let me tell you a secret. There *is* a difference between men and women, a little, tiny one that, I'm afraid, has probably made most of your adult life miserable and will probably continue to make it so till you die. The

difference is simply that women have only really been treated, by that bizarre, Durkheimian abstraction, 'society,' as human beings for the last—oh, say sixty-five years; and then, really, only on the moons; whereas men have had the luxury of such treatment for the last four thousand. The result of this historical anomaly is simply that, on a statistical basis, women are just a little less willing to put up with certain kinds of shit than men—simply because the concept of a certain kind of shit-free Universe is, in that equally bizarre Jungian abstraction, the female 'collective unconscious,' too new and too precious." Lawrence's brows knitted; he frowned at Bron's knotted fists. "Why, I *bet* that's a letter from a lady—I confess, when I was checking for corpses, I had a peek in here and saw the name and the return address. Your problem, you see, is that essentially you are a logical pervert, looking for a woman with a mutually compatible logical perversion. The fact is, the mutual perversion you are looking for is very, very rare—if not nonexistent. You're looking for someone who can enjoy a certain sort of logical masochism. If it were *just* sexual, you'd have no trouble finding a partner at all—as your worldly experience no doubt has already informed you. Hang them from the ceiling, burn their nipples with matches, stick pins in their buttocks and cane them bloody! There're gaggles of women, just as there are gaggles of men, who would be delighted to have a six foot, blond iceberg like you around to play such games with. You can get a list of the places they frequent just by dialing Information. But, though she is a religious fanatic like Mad Mike, who believes that the children of her body are one with the objects of her hand, or a sociopath like poor Alfred, who doesn't quite have a model for anyone, correct or incorrect; be she nun or nymphomaniac, a loud political pamphleteer running around in the u-l sector, or a pillar of society living elegantly on the Ring, or anywhere in between, or any combination, the one thing she is *not* going to do is put up with your hurry-up-and-wait, your do-a-little-tap-dance-while-you-stand-on-your-head, your run-around-in-circles-while-you-walk-a-straight-line, especially when it's out of bed and simply has no hope of pleasurable feedback. Fortunately, your particular perversion today is extremely rare. Oh, I would say maybe one man out of fifty has it—quite amazing, considering that it once was about as common as the ability to grow a beard. Just compare it to some of the other major sexual types: homosexuality, one out of five; bisexuality, three out of five; sadism and masochism, one out of nine; the varieties of fetishism, one out of eight. So you see, at one out of *fifty*, you really are in a difficult situation. And what makes it more difficult—even tragic—is that the corresponding perversion you're searching for in women, thanks to that little historical anomaly, is more like one out of five thousand. Yes, I have a—believe me—platonic curiosity about both male and female victims of this deviation. Yes, I exploit the attendant loneliness of the unfulfilled by offering friendship. Psychic vampirism? Believe me, there's as much of the blood donor about me as there is of Vlad Tepes. I don't know anything about the woman responsible for that—" He nodded toward the crumpled letter—"other than her public reputation. But I've lived a long time. I can make a few speculations about her. Bron, in your terms, she simply doesn't exist. I mean, how can she? You're a logical sadist looking for a logical masochist. But you *are* a logician. If you redefine the relation between P and Not-P beyond a certain point—well, then you just aren't talking about logic any more. All you've done, really, is change the subject."

> "I'm a metalogician," Bron said. "I define and redefine the relation between P and Not-P five hours a day, four days a week. Women don't understand. Faggots don't understand either." (212–214)

As this excerpt demonstrates, a writer may intentionally make her characters commit categorical thinking—bad, good, or a mix—in order to *reveal character.*

A Final Term for Generalization

The most common term for the generalization fallacy when applied to human beings is "stereotyping."

Exercise 3

> Describe yourself with one (and only one) major ROAARS change. In other words, if you describe yourself as being of a different race than you really are, keep this new you at your same age; your physical ability, religion, gender, and sexual orientation should also remain the same. Take four minutes for this exercise.
>
> Afterwards, as you review what you've written, be alert for these things: stereotypes, other changes in your ROAARS traits that seem to stem inevitably from the original change, lack of any noticeable difference beyond the original change, unexpected consequences of the change. Did you find yourself thinking in new ways about the category you theoretically and temporarily "joined"? About the category you theoretically and temporarily "deserted"?

6

Congruence

Using what we call congruence is one good way of establishing ties between a reader (or an author) and a character of one or more different ROAARS characteristics.

The heroine of Nisi's short story "The Tawny Bitch" differs from her creator in a number of ways. "Belle" is a lesbian, whereas Nisi identifies as bisexual. Belle is a minor, and Nisi's a mature woman. Belle is a quadroon; she quantifies precisely the proportions of her African and European ancestry. Nisi's lineage is also largely African and European, but she doesn't know the exact proportions and has no very deep interest in figuring them out. There are other non-ROAARS traits that distance Nisi from her character: Belle is an heiress, while Nisi works for her living, an important class distinction. Belle also identifies strongly as a colonial, a lesser subject of a strong, centralized empire.

These points of dissimilarity regarding its heroine apply to most readers of "The Tawny Bitch," too. The majority will not be lesbians, heiresses, minors, etc.

To help herself as an author connect emotionally to her own heroine and to increase her readers' ability to empathize with her Nisi focused on some specific non-ROAARS characteristics she and her audience might have in common with Belle. She made her a picky eater. She described her as deeply in love—a condition not everyone is in all the time, but one potent enough to remain a vital memory long after the actual experience.

But the main congruency Nisi established between Belle and her creator/consumers was the character's intoxication with words. The story is told primarily via entries in a journal Belle keeps while imprisoned, so her extravagancies of language come through quite clearly in the text, exciting a sympathetic response in those with the same literary inclinations.

In *Sarah Canary,* Karen Joy Fowler uses congruence to show similarities between characters of widely differing ROAARS characteristics. To take one example, though Chin dislikes and fears Indians, he notes that Tom, the Indian he is forced by whites to execute, has very little facial hair, "…no more than Chin himself." (47) To take another example, compare the following passages, the first from the viewpoint of a white suffragette, the second, again, from that of Chin:

"Downstairs, the men were shouting—boisterous, happy sounds. Women were rarely safe when men got drunk and happy together." (166)

"Chinese men were rarely safe when white men got drunk and happy together." (188)

By examining these two passages you can see how Fowler's book simultaneously uses both parallax *and* congruence. The suffragette and Chin face danger from the same sources, and the phrasing underlines this. But unlike Chin, the suffragette disregards racial markers; to her, they're irrelevant to the situation.

Categories All Around Us

Every person belongs to a large number of categories. We doubt there are many individuals who are genuinely *sui generis*. All people have traits and abilities that put them into all sorts of categories or groups—groups that overlap at least some, and potentially most—other groups.

You can be a neurotic white lesbian Zen Buddhist with gorgeous eyes, bad teeth, anorexia, a designer wardrobe that's the envy of Hollywood, a full dog-sled racing team, a condominium in the French Quarter of New Orleans, a summer home on the coast of Maine.... Some of these are ROAARS traits, and some are not. Some are consistent with one another or with stereotypes attributed to identification with a particular group. Others are diametrically opposed to those stereotypes or completely unrelated to the rest of these traits. One trait may imply membership in a different economic class than another does—a non-ROAARS distinction of important though often unconscious consideration.

The same multi-group/cross-group traits should be true of your characters. Even your secondary characters.

Generally, a secondary character has one main character trait. However, a secondary character shouldn't *be* that one trait exclusively. Neither should all the secondary character's few illustrated traits point to the same ROAARS category. That makes a stereotype of even the most minor of "bit players."

For example, don't make a secondary character's main trait be his gayness and then portray him as a bitchy, effeminate San Francisco florist with a great collection of disco-diva CDs. There's nothing wrong with a character's being gay, or effeminate, or a florist, or a disco fan, or a San Francisco resident. But when every trait you ascribe to a character points to the same group, you're just promoting a widely-held stereotype.

How about a secondary character who's a bitchy, straight florist who has a pet house rabbit and thinks rap music has gone way downhill since Public Enemy's third CD? Or who's an African-American computer programmer and classical oboist?

It's not often we run across these characters in fiction—but they're believable. Even if they're unusual, they're believable. And don't you find such characters more interesting than common stereotypes?

Do You Remember When? Congruence and Change

Do you remember when it used to be remarkable for a male writer to write believable, complex woman characters? Did you, perhaps, tell all the female readers you knew, and perhaps even all the male readers, about this stereotype-shattering male writer?

That has changed. Nowadays, we are more likely to remark on instances in which a male writer creates unbelievable, one-dimensional female characters.

For another example of progress in this area, we recommend reading Chan Davis's 1949 essay "Critique and Proposals" discussing stereotypes in science fiction. Davis's concerns were more limited in their scope than ours, yet knowledgeable genre readers will be able to see how many of his suggestions had an impact on the field.

We change. Our culture changes. Someday, we hope, we will not see differences like skin color as barriers to believable characterization—or as barriers to writing about people of other races. Someday, perhaps, we may only see our virtual reality representations as differences.

Exercise 4

Create a list of non-ROAARS traits for the ROAARS character from Exercise 2. Alternatively, create the list for an other-ROAARS character from your own fiction, or for one you were thinking of writing. Take one minute to do this.

When you have the list, look it over. Do all the non-ROAARS traits point to identification with one particular ROAARS category? Do they contradict or reinforce each other? Do they include hobbies, physical characteristics, geographical origins, hopes, education, employment? Try this again, with other characters, as many times as you like.

Exercise 5

Once more, here's an exercise you'll find a lot more valuable when you do it with a partner or when you at least get an interested bystander to help you out. You'll also need at least two magazines.

You and your partner should select two pictures from the magazines. Each picture should be primarily of one person. When both of you have your selections ready, hand them over to each other. (If you're doing this alone, ask a friend who's not participating to pick the pictures for you—it's important that you don't select the material for yourself or even see it before you begin writing about it. If you and your exercise partner are doing this via email, try to send each other jpgs or URLs for photos available over the internet.)

Next, write a description of the people in the two pictures in terms of how they differ from one another. Take three minutes for this description.

Now describe the pictures in terms of how the people they portray are alike. Take three minutes for this description, too.

As always, it's worth taking time after completing the exercise to consider what you've been through. Was one description harder to write than the other? If so, which? Did the people in the pictures remind you of anyone in real life or in the fiction you've read or created? Did you identify more strongly with one of them than with the other?

7

Unintended and Intended Associations and Resonances

Unintended associations and resonances are the bane of a writer's existence; they're particularly pernicious when it comes to writing the other.

An association is the simple one-to-one connection of two ideas. You may deliberately make associations, or your readers may bring them to your work, creating an unanticipated relationship between your chosen setting (or some other story element) and an idea you believed entirely foreign to it.

Resonance involves a complex of ideas that reinforce and highlight one another through the multiplicity of their connections.

Intended or not, associations and resonances greatly influence the ideas or feelings imparted by a piece of fiction: the mood, the underlying meaning, the unstated burden of the story. Because they are inexplicit, they're difficult to control. They can partake of the author's conscious and unconscious input but draw their primary power from the input of your audience. When we deal with resonances and associations arising from social issues such as ROAARS traits, much of what we're working with derives from the social surround in which a text is read.

Controlling resonances and associations involving ROAARS requires authors to combine difficulty of technique with challenging—disturbing—even explosive content.

Both Nisi and Cynthia attended the 1992 session of the Clarion West Writers Workshop. As mentioned earlier, a classmate's comment spurred Nisi to write the essay that eventually grew into the *Writing the Other* class and then this guide. That session of Clarion West also provided an unforgettable example of unfortunate, unintended resonance with ROAARS implications.

The format of the Clarion workshops focuses on critiquing short stories written in situ. One such story depicted a man with a German surname who imprisoned children in his basement and tortured them. Nearly every one of the author's twenty classmates saw this character's name as an intentional evocation of Nazism and the Holocaust and interpreted the story on the basis of that assumption. Faced with several similar misinterpretations of his work during his classmates' verbal presentation of their critiques, the chagrined author was forced to admit that he'd picked the German surname at random.

How could the author have avoided giving his readers the erroneous impression that they were reading a modern Nazi fable? How can you avoid and disarm similar unintended resonances or associations in your own work?

Actually, Nisi and Cindy's classmate was on the right path. Remember, his readers at this point were colleagues, not the general public. Writing is considered speech; it helps to have more than one person considering what you've said—*before* publication.

Bearing in mind that thoughtful pre-publication critique is your best defense against unintended resonances and associations, there are some steps you can take to ensure receiving helpful critiques—and some steps you can skip. To begin with, it's worth noting that not all those who felt the story's resonance with the Nazi Holocaust were Jews or descendants of other groups victimized by the Holocaust. That's good, because it means you don't have to have a preconceived idea about who you may be unintentionally offending. And you don't have to run your manuscript by people with exactly the same ROAARS traits as your characters. What you need is a pool of reasonably intelligent, well-informed, and articulate readers.

Of course, diversity of any sort—especially of ROAARS traits—will increase your readers' ability to contribute helpful feedback to you. It will not, however, prevent you from making mistakes that see print.

Learning boils down to making mistakes, seeing what you've done wrong, and making corrections. If you're going to be a good writer, if you're going to improve, you mustn't flinch from this process.

Do your best. Eventually, you'll figure out how to make your best better.

Intended Resonances: Not Always a Good Idea

Consciously *creating* a resonance doesn't guarantee the resonance will be a good idea.

A few years ago, Cynthia read Julie Smith's mystery novel *82 Desire*. In this novel, an important character was christened, through the trickery of a nasty white doctor, with the name Urethra.

The white author made this black character the most interesting and likeable person in the novel. The author also recognized that she had to make this astonishing christening the defining moment of the unfortunate woman's life.

While the word urethra is in and of itself a perfectly legitimate anatomical term, in this context (as the name of an African American female) it carries the following associations: ignorance of the word's primary usage; mispronunciation of the name of the well-known singer Aretha Franklin; and through the urethra's connection to urine and other excreta, the misconception that African Americans are dirtier than whites (as exampled by the reluctance of Ivory Soap to sponsor the appearances of another well-known singer, Billy Holliday).

Given all this, how many readers are going to keep reading after the revelation of the character's wildly offensive first name?

The novel is a better-than-average mystery, but Cynthia has never recommended it to anyone on the assumption that most readers will have a bad reaction to the intended resonance of Urethra's name. Too, Nisi has never expressed an interest in reading *82 Desire*: quite the opposite.

Lincoln Child's suspense thriller *Utopia* offers another example of an intended, yet unfortunate, resonance.

In the novel, Utopia is a gigantic theme park with thousands of employees and 65,000 visitors a day. Yet everyone in the novel has a last name that's Anglo-Saxon, Irish, or German. Would you believe that nobody with a Spanish, Italian, Japanese, or Nigerian surname visits Disneyland? Of course you wouldn't.

But we exaggerate—slightly. There are *some* characters not of WASP, Irish, or German descent. These characters are an Asian love interest; an "almond-eyed" terrorist (race unspecified, but obviously he's "foreign"); and a coke addict with tight-curled hair whose drug habit is used to blackmail him into betraying the theme park's security measures.

The resonances invoked by the last character's traits are intentional. We're clearly supposed to recognize him as a coke-snorting, spineless black man.

But being coy about race or other ROAARS categories doesn't make a negative resonance positive, especially when the character is the only member of his/her group—or the only member of *any* minority ROAARS classification—in the novel.

An easy way to disarm this kind of resonance is to have more than one or two members of a particular ROAARS classification in your novel or novella, and to have several different minorities represented. If Child's novel had reflected in microcosm the normal diversity of a theme park, he'd have had African-American and "foreign" characters who behaved well, and not just the African-American and "foreign" characters who behaved badly. You don't want to reproduce Child's error.

Some stories, novels, and movies have small casts and/or homogeneous settings that will preclude your being able to introduce much diversity. That's fine. There's no point in introducing diversity when it's unlikely or impossible. When Cynthia watched the movie *Mooseport*, she quickly and accurately deduced the small-town-Maine-set movie was not filmed in Maine because it had too many black characters. When researching her nonfiction book *Nickeled and Dimed: On (Not) Getting By in America*, Barbara Ehrenreich investigated minimum-wage existence in Maine because no one there would notice a poor white woman scrubbing toilets. (51) Much of Maine is poor, and 96.9% of Maine is white (http://factfinder.census.gov/).

And yet, Maine has diversity, even in its smallest villages. Not all homosexual small-town Mainers leave their small towns. Some Mainers need wheelchairs. There are Mainers taller, shorter, fatter, skinnier, richer, poorer, healthier, and less healthy than the perceived American "average." By the standards of her father's WASPy Maine hometown (pop. 300), Cynthia is the product of a mixed marriage: her mother is of French descent. And in Maine's isolated, ethnically homogeneous Washington County, a Mexican grocery recently opened. Even a brief story set in Maine can include diversity—just not the same kinds of diversity as those kinds likely to be found in Miami, Detroit, San Jose, Santa Fe, or Billings.

When you write a novel or script which, like *Utopia*, features a large cast in a multi-cultural American setting, reflect that diversity of heritage, nationality, and sexual orientation. Even particularly unobservant members of the unmarked state may notice if 99.9% of your characters are straight whites.

Exercise 6

You can use an excerpt from your own writing as the basis for this exercise, or you can select something from the work of another author.

Find a scene in which the story's main character encounters someone else. Rewrite that scene so that the secondary character encountered differs in one ROAARS characteristic from the original version. Take five minutes for this exercise if you're typing it; eight if you're writing longhand.

When you're done, re-read what you've come up with. How does it differ from the original scene? Is it stronger? Weaker? More or less plausible?

Exercise 7

Now, from this same manuscript, story, or novel, pick another scene in which the main character appears and rewrite it, making a change in this main character's ROAARS characteristics identical to the change you made for the secondary character in Exercise 6. Give yourself four minutes; six if you're writing longhand.

As you consider the new scene you've come up with, ask yourself the same questions you asked after Exercise 6. You may also want to think about which of these two exercises was easier or whether doing one made it easier to do the other.

8

Don't Do This!

In this section we examine just a few of the many, many mistakes it's possible to make as we write about characters of different ROAARS characteristics from our own. When it comes to writing the other, we've all got a lot to learn. Fortunately, the errors of writers who have attempted to portray those of other ROAARS characteristics are available as examples that we strongly advise you NOT to follow. As the Yoruba saying has it, "If we stand tall, it's because we stand on the shoulders of our ancestors." Don't be afraid to get a boost up from your literary forebears and profit from the lessons to be learned from what they've done; the worlds you create and the one we actually live in will all benefit greatly.

"The Dark Hordes Attacked"

And they usually attacked pseudo-Celts and pseudo-Vikings.

This is such a hoary fantasy cliché it doesn't need much discussion. If you find yourself casting heroes and villains (whether as individuals or groups) exclusively along lines of color, religion, sexual orientation, or the like, it's time to re-think your approach.

Example: S.M. Stirling's novella "Shikari in Galveston" (*Worlds that Weren't*, edited by Harry Turtledove) has a large cast with a tough, believable warrior woman. But all the blacks are cannibals, safari bearers, or corpses. And the cannibals are the hapless tools of a white man!

Here Stirling is deliberately working in the tradition of Robert E. Howard, Edgar Rice Burroughs, and H. Rider Haggard, old-fashioned colonialist adventure-fiction authors. Yet for all their problems, these decades-dead white fellows managed to create black characters far more diverse, differentiated, and believable than those of the modern-day author.

Glory Syndrome

Common in Hollywood, but not unknown to print fiction. In this scenario, the movie/story pivots around the concerns central to those far removed from the unmarked state (say, slavery for example), but the plot is all about how the issue affects those in the unmarked state (say, American whites.)

This isn't strictly an error, but it's getting old. If you're writing about American slavery, why not focus on the people it affects most? It's not like you can't show the ways it affects whites, too.

Example: *Glory* (which is a good movie—it's just about the wrong people).

Counter-Examples: Spike Lee's movie *Do the Right Thing* and Steven Barnes's alternate-history novels *Lion's Blood* and *Zulu Heart*.

Sidekicks-R-Us

The straight, white, usually male main character has a best friend of a significantly different ROAARS categorization, and that friend exists primarily to validate the hipness of the main character.

Cynthia didn't see the TV series, but the novels she read in Robert B. Parker's *Spenser* detective series clearly used the character of the calm, collected, criminal black man Hawk to function as a "coolness" indicator for the white hero, Spenser.

Using marked-state characters to lend cachet to unmarked heroes, thus bringing them closer to the marked state, is such a cliché that the TV comedy show *In Living Color* parodied it (and specifically the *Lethal Weapon* movies) with a joke TV show called "Sidekick."

A particularly weak variation on Sidekickism is to have just one to three black characters in the novel/movie, who exist only as bit-players: cops or bodyguards or the like. Alternatively, a minority character may have a better role (like that of a fellow soldier or fighter pilot in a war movie), but he (it's usually a *he*) is soon killed off, apparently because the author can't think of anything else to do with the poor guy. "There!" you can hear the writer thinking. "I promoted diversity. Now, on with the real story!"

The sidekick's fatal marked state isn't always related to ROAARS traits. A happy relationship or family life leads to sidekick death frequently enough to be parodied in the 1991 move *Hot Shots*: white fighter pilot Pete Thompson is so happy about his wife and kids that all the other pilots call him "Dead Meat"—and he's barely introduced before he's killed.

Laurell K. Hamilton's *Cerulean Sins* displays a couple of variations of Sidekickism.

Hamilton does create sympathetic, complex gay, bisexual, and polyamorous characters, and she has also come up with an interesting and effective way to examine ROAARS classifications, category, and the unmarked state. Her alternate Earth is partly populated by vampires, werewolves, and other were-beasts—intelligent beings who have recently won legal rights in the US but still face prejudice and hatred.

There is, however, a major problem with *Cerulean Sins.* The book is set in St. Louis, a midwestern US city known for its proportionately large black population, and despite its sizeable cast, only three black characters appear in the whole novel. Any reader who knows anything about race in the US will ask, "So where did all the dark-skinned people go?" One of the three black characters is a werewolf bodyguard for the main character's ex-lover. The other two are foreign vampires who speak an unknown language. They are bodyguards for the antagonists, and they exist only to be killed—repeatedly. Since they're vampires, it takes at least two attempts to make them truly, permanently dead.

Talk about "Dead Meat"!

Counter-Example: The Hap & Leonard mystery/suspense novels of Joe R. Lansdale. In this series, the relationship between marked- and unmarked-state characters is one of equals; neither exists to prove anything about the other.

Subtle Victimization

You know you're in the presence of this error when everyone's beautifully and insightfully characterized; but the black characters are all victims and/or minor criminals, and power remains in the hands of the power elite (almost exclusively straight and white though not all-male anymore).

James Lee Burke is an excellent author, but his Dave Robichaux detective novel *Purple Cane Road*, which is intelligently sympathetic to the effects of racism in Louisiana, shows signs of this problem. When you get right down to brass tacks, in Burke's novel the whites (some of them; not nearly all) have a monopoly on power and the blacks are victims.

The only black cop is a dispatcher—he's in no position to right wrongs or even to do any "policing."

This book does *not* commit the "Great White Father" error of having a straight white guy fix the blacks' or other minority-ROAARS status characters' problems. No one is able to right the terrible wrong done to an unjustly imprisoned black woman.

That is realistic.

But it is not particularly realistic that every black character in a novel is powerless and that almost every one is a victim. No marked-status member of any ROAARS classification is always powerless. And blacks/gays/etc. aren't always victims.

Counter-Example: The Easy Rawlins mystery/detective novels by Walter Mosley.

In this series we have black heroes and villains, white good guys and bad guys. There are enormous problems. But the blacks solve their own problems, and sometimes white folks' problems as well.

Patronizing Romanticizations

Another category of error encompasses the Noble Savage and other imaginary figures. This sort of character arises when the author fetishizes difference to such an extent that nothing is allowed to detract from it or diffuse it. The traits ascribed to the marked state may be seen as admirable or reprehensible, but they're presented to readers in the simplest form possible.

Examples: James P. Hogan's "Madam Butterfly" beautifully illustrates the so-called "Butterfly Effect," the part of Chaos Theory that explains how small changes in initial conditions can cause big consequences down the road. But he makes his first viewpoint character, an elderly Japanese woman, unbelievably naïve about the world around her. In Chifumi Shimoto's eyes, her country is just "...a province in some vaster scheme that she [doesn't] understand..." (687) The struggle between Earth's government and the Libertarian-leaning miners in the outer system where her son lives is beyond her: "She had never understood it..." (688)

Because the story is set in a fairly near future—sometime in the next 100 years—Chifumi's childhood in a remote mountain valley would have to have taken place in the first decade of the twenty-first century, at the earliest—which means this valley, while remote, couldn't have been completely isolated. Almost no place can be these days, and certainly no place in Japan. Also, she has been living in a sophisticated urban center, Tokyo, for most of her life—decades, presumably. So why does this woman know nothing of world affairs?

Perhaps Hogan cast her as ignorant because she reveres a mountain spirit called Kyo. Chifumi's Kyo-reverence is intrinsic to the plot, but as a real life nature-spirit worshipper, Nisi can testify that ignorance and naiveté are not prerequisites for this particular variety of the religious experience.

Far more blatant romanticization occurs in "Belief," by P.D. Cacek. Samuel, an elderly black man dressed in rags, apparently an ex-slave (he mentions his former "massa"), guides a newly-killed soldier through Heaven. The soldier realizes that each dead soul creates its own version of the place when Samuel gives him a piece of fresh sugar cane. Holding Samuel's hand, he sees the black man's Heaven: a massive field of sugar cane and a small cabin by a fishpond. The author, in other words, portrays the height of Samuel's ambition as that of owning a better grade of shack than the slave quarters he occupied during life—located conveniently close to a loving reproduction of the site where he labored dawn till dusk. New clothes free of holes and tatters aren't actually desired, let alone required. These simple people have such simple needs…

But Maybe Someone Really Did Say That…

Sometimes an offensive or erroneous representation of a person of a different ROAARS classification springs from the author's own experience.

As we all know, there's a difference between recounting the facts and telling the truth. Objectivity is problematic in journalism; and when it comes to fiction, it's a moot point. Though someone may have said or done something that accords with your view of those of a different ROAARS classification, the act of selecting this event for representation in your work moves it from the realm of the objective to that of the subjective.

You noticed it. You decided it was important. You placed it in a certain context. You scripted your other characters' reactions to it. You're trying to imbue it with meaning, and there's no escaping your responsibility for that, whether or not the attempt is successful.

Just because you've based what you've written on something that truly did occur doesn't mean that what you've written is the truth. Your story will benefit from your examination of the implications of what you've written, from the feedback you receive on its impact, from your consideration of how typical it may be, and from your questioning of what other parts of the picture you may have missed.

Example: Midway through Margaret Mitchell's *Gone With the Wind*, the author paints a picture of Reconstruction as an irresponsible free-for-all in which childlike "darkies" are lured from the countryside to urban dens of vice, then abandoned. From their seats on the curbs of city streets, these rustic innocents cry out to passing white women to "...write my old Marster down in Fayette County dat Ah's up hyah....'Fo' Gawd, Ah done got nuff of dis freedom!" (646)

When Nisi complained to another African American woman about this scene, the woman responded that it was at least theoretically possible that a freed slave could have had this reaction. That doesn't make Mitchell's artistic choice to spotlight a plea to be re-enslaved less reprehensible or more plausible.

Disrespectful Dialect

Elsewhere in this book, in the essay "Appropriate Cultural Appropriation," Nisi states that "all speech is (arguably) made in one or another dialect; in attempting accurate transcription of any particular version of English, we mark it as nonstandard and in some sense deprivilege it." (92) If your goal is to connect rather than distance your reader from what you're writing, you need to think carefully about how you represent your characters' speech. Dialect is very much a verbal analogue of the marked state, and because of this its use can be a bad move.

Even worse than transcribing speech with overly zealous accuracy, however, is careless or inaccurate transcription. Many of your readers will be blown completely out of whatever milieu you wished to establish. Those belonging to or deeply familiar with the ROAARS classification you're supposedly representing will distrust everything else you attempt to show them; those only slightly acquainted with it may be distracted from the point you want to make, or the story you're trying to tell, as they puzzle over what Miz So-an-so said: Was that a typo? A word they ought to look up in their dictionary? Do people really talk like that? Where and when? And why?

We're not saying that reproducing colloquial speech patterns is a mistake—simply that it is difficult to do well and can *lead to* mistakes.

Examples: Turning again to Cacek's "Belief," we find numerous improbable sentences attributed to the formerly enslaved Samuel. Appraising the dead soldier he says, "Whoo-wee, will yor lookit all dem medals." (230) When the two come across a group of children, he comments, "It be hard t'see dem so young, but you gotta know dey be happy here. Some o' 'em even happier den when dey was breathin'." (238) Giving the soldier a piece of fruit, Samuel jokes that "Yesshur, ol' Chancy gots t'have da chance t'eats dat peach. Yesshur." (239)

"Yesshur" is repeated. Not a typo, then. So is "yor" "you?" Are both "dem" and "'em" "them?" Why the distinction? And "da" is filling in for "the"; perhaps it ought to be pronounced "duh" rather than "dah"?

Even after all this processing, Samuel's speech sounds like no one else's—at least no one else that Nisi has ever heard. You don't want your readers to have to work this hard, and you don't want them to be this dissatisfied with the results of their efforts.

The Saintly Victim

You commit this *faux pas* when you emphasize the evil of racism, sexism, child abuse, murder—whatever!—by increasing the innocence of the victim. For example, when you show that child abuse is wrong by making your child victim spotlessly perfect. This child has never stolen a cookie—never even given it a thought!

Yeah, right.

Don't create a blameless victim so good that Mother Theresa looks Hell-bound in comparison. For that matter, you needn't make the victim particularly good at all. Evil behavior is evil behavior. Gay-bashing is wrong, and it doesn't matter if the victim was trying to force his unwanted attentions on the man who beat him up.

Counter-Example: "Night They Missed the Horror Show" by Joe R. Lansdale (Schow 1988).

The main character and his buddy are racist whites who rescue a black classmate, their quarterback, from violent rival teammates who find him when his car breaks down. It turns out the quarterback stole the car. He was not free of sin, though of course he didn't deserve to be attacked by the rival team.

"Don't Go There!"

If you do, you'll lose almost all your readers.

In addition to the previously mentioned unfortunately-named character in Julie Smith's mystery novel *82 Desire*, here are a couple of other "places" not to go:

"Hitler was a good guy, just misunderstood." As with the "dark hordes," there's no real need to elaborate on this theme. It's a guaranteed loser. Trust us on this one.

"The rape victim who falls in love with her/his rapist." We're willing to believe this happens in real life, but

(a) not very often, and (b) we don't care. We won't read any further. Neither will many other readers.

Conclusion

You Can Do It!

If you've just read the preceding section, you may be feeling a little discouraged right now. There are so many ways to go wrong. You'll no doubt be able to think of some on your own that we haven't mentioned.

Remember, though, that the possibility of failure is no excuse for not making the attempt.

At this point, you're much better prepared to succeed than you were when you first started reading this guide. You have techniques. You have examples. You have new ways of talking about what you want to do, new ways of seeing characters, of seeing otherness.

And you know that you're not alone. You are one of many writers seeking to improve the stories we tell each other by making them about all of us, in all of our glorious differences. Past students of *Writing the Other* workshops have stayed in touch, offering one another help and constructive criticism. If you'd like to contact fellow readers of this guide in a similar spirit, you can do so through the *Writing the Other* website: www.writingtheother.com.

You may also find support for this aspect of your work among people you already know. Share this guide with them. Do the exercises together. Pool your knowledge. If you'd like to have us come to your area and present the live version of the workshop, you can contact us via the website, at the URL above.

As you put your new Writing the Other tools to use, they'll sharpen, and your awareness of how best to employ them will expand. You've reached the end of this guide, but you're at the beginning of an exciting new phase in your work. Congratulations on getting off to a good start!

Exercise 8

Create a list of resource people with whom you're acquainted. Include people of different ROAARS characteristics than your own, people with non-ROAARS differences, people whose judgment, taste, and insight you respect. Take two minutes to compile your list.

As you review the results of this final exercise, think about how you can connect with these people in ways that will improve your writing in the areas we've covered. Your current relationships with them may well range from bare acquaintance to marriage, and this will affect the kind of help you'll ask of them, as well as how you'll compensate them for their help. They may be eager to assist you. They may prefer to refer you to someone else. Or they may disagree entirely with any attempts at writing the other.

There's one way to find out.

Try it.

Works Cited

Barnes, Steven. *Lion's Blood.* New York, NY, Aspect/Warner, 2002.

———. *Zulu Heart.* New York, NY, Warner, 2003.

Burke, James Lee. *Purple Cane Road: A Novel.* New York, NY, Doubleday, 2000.

Cacek, P.D. "Belief." Al Sarrantonio, ed., *Redshift: Extreme Visions of Speculative Fiction.* New York, NY, Roc, 2001.

Cannavo, S. *Think to Win: The Power of Logic in Everyday Life.* Amherst, NY, Prometheus Books, 1998, 232.

Child, Lincoln. *Utopia.* New York, NY, Doubleday, 2004.

Davis, Chan. "Critique and Proposals," <http://www.pseudopodium.org/repress/chandler-davis/critique-1949.html>, 1949.

Delany, Samuel R. *Dhalgren.* New York, NY, Bantam, 1975.

———. *Triton: An Ambiguous Heterotopia.* New York, NY, Bantam Spectra, 1976. As *Trouble on Triton: An Ambiguous Heterotopia.* Hanover, NH, Wesleyan University Press/University Press of New England, 1996.

Do the Right Thing. Produced and directed by Spike Lee. 120 min. Universal Pictures, 1989. DVD/Videocassette.

Egan, Greg. "Wang's Carpet." Bear, Greg, ed., *New Legends.* New York, NY, Tor, 1995.

Ehrenreich, Barbara. *Nickel and Dimed: On (Not) Getting By in America.* New York, NY, Metropolitan Books, 2001.

Fowler, Karen Joy. *Sarah Canary.* New York, NY, H. Holt, 1991.

Glory. Produced by Freddie Fields, Pieter Jan Brugge, and Ray Herbeck Jr., and director by Edward Zwick.

122 min. Columbia/Tri-Star Studios, 1989. DVD/Videocassette.

Hamilton, Laurell K. *Cerulean Sins*. New York, NY, Berkley, 2003.

Hardman, M.J. Comments made in person during session of "Writing the Other" workshop, Madison, Wisconsin, May 25, 2003.

Hogan, James P. "Madame Butterfly." Brad Linaweaver and Edward E. Kramer, eds., *Free Space*. New York, NY, Tor, 1997.

Hot Shots! Produced by William Badalato and directed by Jim Abrahams. 83 min. Twentieth Century Fox, 1991. DVD/Videocassette.

In Living Color. Produced by Keenan Ivory Wayans. Fox TV, 1990-1994. DVD.

Lansdale, Joe R. "Night They Missed the Horror Show." Schow, David J., ed., *Silver Scream*. Arlington Heights, IL, Dark Harvest Press, 1988.

——. *Savage Season* et seq [Hap & Leonard mystery series]. Shingletown, CA, Mark V. Ziesing, 1990.

Lethal Weapon. Produced by Joel Silver and Richard Donner, and directed by Richard Donner. 110 min. Warner Studios, 1987. DVD/Videocassette.

Mitchell, Margaret. *Gone With the Wind*. New York, NY, Avon Books, 1973.

Mosley, Walter. *Devil in a Blue Dress* et seq [Easy Rawlins mystery series]. New York, NY, W.W. Norton & Company, 1990.

Parker, Robert B. *Promised Land* et seq [Spenser mystery series]. Boston, MA, Houghton/Mifflin, 1976.

Peters, William. *A Class Divided: Then and Now*. New Haven, CT, Yale University Press, 1987.

Petrie, Donald, director; Richardson, Doug, story; Schulman, Tom, screenplay. *Welcome to Mooseport.* Beverly Hills, CA, Twentieth Century Fox, 2004.

Shawl, Nisi. "The Tawny Bitch." Hopkinson, Nalo, ed., *Mojo: Conjure Stories.* New York, NY, Warner, 2003.

Smith, Julie. *82 Desire: A Skip Langdon Novel.* New York, NY, Fawcett Columbine, 1998.

Steinbeck, John. *Travels with Charley.* New York, NY, Viking Press, 1962.

Stirling, S.M. "Shikari in Galveston." Harry Turtledove, ed., *Worlds that Weren't.* New York, NY, Roc, 2002.

Thomas, Sheree R., ed. *Dark Matter.* New York, NY, Aspect/Warner, 2000.

———. *Dark Matter 2: Reading the Bones.* New York, NY, Aspect/Warner, 2004.

Zettel, Sarah. *Fool's War.* New York, NY, Aspect/Warner, 1997.

Recommended Reading/Viewing

Anonymous. *Black People Love Us.* <http://www.blackpeopleloveus.com>.

Auel, Jean M. *The Clan of the Cave Bear: A Novel.* New York, NY, Crown, 1980.

Barnes, Steven. *Lion's Blood.* New York, NY, Aspect/Warner, 2002.

———. *Zulu Heart.* New York, NY, Warner, 2003.

Baker, Kyle. *The Cowboy Wally Show.* New York, NY, Dolphin/Doubleday, 1988.

———. *I Die at Midnight.* New York, NY, Vertigo/DC Comics, 2000.

———. *Why I Hate Saturn.* New York, NY, Piranha Press, 1990.

———. *You Are Here.* New York, NY, Vertigo/DC Comics, 1999.

Delany, Samuel R. *Dhalgren.* New York, NY, Bantam, 1975.

———. *Triton: An Ambiguous Heterotopia.* New York, NY, Bantam Spectra, 1976. As *Trouble on Triton: An Ambiguous Heterotopia.* Hanover, NH, Wesleyan University Press/University Press of New England, 1996.

Do the Right Thing. Produced and directed by Spike Lee. 120 min. Universal Pictures, 1989. DVD/Videocassette.

Egan, Greg. *Schild's Ladder.* New York, NY, EOS/Avon, 2002.

———. "Wang's Carpet" (*The Hard SF Renaissance*, edited by David G. Hartwell & Kathryn Cramer)

Fowler, Karen Joy. *Sarah Canary.* New York, NY, H. Holt, 1991.

———. *Sister Noon.* New York, NY, G.P. Putnam's Sons, 2001.

———. "What I Didn't See." SciFiction, July 2002, <http://www.scifi.com/scifiction/originals/originals_archive/fowler/>.

Frost, Gregory. "The Prowl." Hopkinson, Nalo, ed., *Mojo: Conjure Stories.* New York, NY, Warner, 2003.

Griffith, Nicola & Pagel, Stephen, eds. *Bending the Landscape: Fantasy.* Clarkston, GA, Borealis/White Wolf Publishing, 1996.

———. *Bending the Landscape: Horror.* Woodstock, NY, The Overlook Press, 2001.

———. *Bending the Landscape: Science Fiction.* Woodstock, NY, The Overlook Press, 1998.

Hannibal. Produced by Dino De Laurentiis, Martha De Laurentiis, and Ridley Scott, and directed by Ridley Scott. 131 min. MGM/UA, 2001. DVD/Videocassette.

Harris, Thomas, *The Silence of the Lambs.* New York, NY, St. Martins Press, 1988.

Hopkinson, Nalo, ed. *Mojo: Conjure Stories.* New York, NY, Warner, 2003.

Lansdale, Joe R. *Savage Season* et seq [Hap & Leonard mystery series]. Shingletown, CA, Mark V. Ziesing, 1990.

———. "Night They Missed the Horror Show." Schow, David J., ed., *Silver Scream.* Arlington Heights, IL, Dark Harvest Press, 1988.

McHugh, Maureen F. *China Mountain Zhang.* New York, NY, Tor, 1992.

———. *Mission Child.* New York, NY, EOS/Avon, 1998.

McIntyre, Vonda N. *The Moon and the Sun.* New York, NY, Pocket, 1997.

Mosley, Walter. *Devil in a Blue Dress* et seq [Easy Rawlins mystery series]. New York, NY, W.W. Norton & Company, 1990.

Ruff, Matt. *Sewer, Gas & Electric.* Atlantic Monthly Press, 1997.

Shawl, Nisi. "The Tawny Bitch." Hopkinson, Nalo, ed., *Mojo: Conjure Stories.* New York, NY, Warner, 2003.

Smith, Alexander McCall. *The No. 1 Ladies' Detective Agency.* Cape Town, South Africa, D. Philip, 1998. New York, NY, Anchor, 2002.

Something's Gotta Give. Produced by Bruce Block (II), Nancy Meyers, and Suzanne Farwell, and directed by Nancy Meyers. 123 min. Columbia/Tri-Star Studios, 2003. DVD/Videocassette.

Sterling, Bruce, "Maneki Neko." *The Magazine of Fantasy & Science Fiction*, May 1998. *A Good Old-Fashioned Future*, New York, NY, Bantam, 1999.

The Silence of the Lambs. Produced by Edward Saxon, Kenneth Utt, and Ron Bozman, and directed by Jonathan Demme. 120 min. Orion Studios, 1991. DVD/Videocassette.

Thomas, Sheree R., editor. *Dark Matter*; *Dark Matter 2: Reading the Bones.*

Ward, Cynthia. "The Lost Homeland." Griffith, Nicola & Pagel, Stephen, eds., *Bending the Landscape: Horror.* Woodstock, NY, Overlook Press, 2001.

Zettel, Sarah. *Fool's War.* New York, NY, Aspect/Warner, 1997.

Mixed

Burke, James Lee. *Purple Cane Road: A Novel.* New York, NY, Doubleday, 2000.

Gibson, William. *Count Zero.* New York, NY, Arbor House, 1986.

———. *Neuromancer.* New York, NY, Ace, 1984.

Glory. Produced by Freddie Fields, Pieter Jan Brugge, and Ray Herbeck Jr., and director by Edward Zwick. 122 min. Columbia/Tri-Star Studios, 1989. DVD/Videocassette.

Hamilton, Laurell K. *Cerulean Sins.* New York, NY, Berkley, 2003.

Lethal Weapon. Produced by Joel Silver and Richard Donner, and directed by Richard Donner. 110 min. Warner Studios, 1987. DVD/Videocassette.

Parker, Robert B. *Promised Land* et seq [Spenser mystery series]. Boston, MA, Houghton/Mifflin, 1976.

Smith, Julie. *82 Desire: A Skip Langdon Novel.* New York, NY, Fawcett Columbine, 1998.

Stirling, S.M. *Against the Tide of Years.* New York, NY, Roc, 1999.

———. *Island in the Sea of Time.* New York, NY, Roc, 1998.

———. *On the Oceans of Eternity.* New York, NY, Roc, 2000.

———. "Shikari in Galveston." Harry Turtledove, ed., *Worlds that Weren't.* New York, NY, Roc, 2002.

Beautiful Strangers: Transracial Writing for the Sincere

by Nisi Shawl

"I'd never write about a person from a different ethnic background. The whole story would probably be full of horrible stereotypes and racist slurs."

Amy closed her mouth, and mine dropped open. Luckily, I was seated when my friend made this statement, but the lawn chair must have sagged visibly with the weight of my disbelief. My own classmate excluding all other ethnic types from her creative universe!

I think this sort of misguided caution is the source of a lot of sf's monochrome futures. You know the ones I mean, where some nameless and never discussed plague has mysteriously killed off everyone with more than a hint of melanin in their skin. I wonder sometimes what kind of career I'd have if I followed suit with tales of stalwart Space Negroes and an unexplained absence of whites.

But of course I don't. I boldly write about people from other backgrounds, just as many of the field's best authors do. Suzie McKee Charnas, Bruce Sterling, and Sarah Zettel have all produced wonderful transracial characters, as I show in examples below. Before getting into their work, though, let's discuss how to prepare for your own.

If you want to go beyond the level of just assigning different skin tones and heritages to random characters, you're going to have to do some research. Because yes, all people are the same, but they're also quite different. For now, we'll set aside the argument that race is an artificial construct and concentrate on how someone outside a minority group can gain enough knowledge of the group's common traits to realistically represent one of its members.

Reading's a very non-confrontational way to do this. Be sure, though, if you choose this route, to use as many primary sources as possible. If researching a story about first contact between a stranded explorer from Aldeberan and a runaway slave, for example, you'd do much better reading *The Life & Times of Frederick Douglass* than *Uncle Tom's Cabin.* The latter is an important and moving book. But not only is it a work of fiction, it was written by a non-slave; therefore, it's a step further removed from the authentic experience you need.

Websites on minority culture abound. Any half-decent search engine will bring up a freighter's worth of URLs on African-Americans, for instance, and at least a page or two on lesser-known groups.

For a less cerebral approach, check out nearby ethnic history museums. Art collections, historical dioramas, anthropological displays, and so on can provide you with strong visuals. Some are interactive and allow you to pick up a few aural and tactile sensations as well. For locations, look under "Museums" in the yellow pages, or consult a travel guide for your area.

When it comes to finding more contemporary material, magazines help. I also strongly recommend shopping trips, night-clubbing, and restaurant hopping. Take a walk on the wild side. Do you feel like a tourist? Uncomfortable? Well, you are one, and you need to know what it's like to be conspicuous. If your character's a minority, she or he will be quite familiar with the sensation. Bruce Sterling once told me that alienation is an essential part of any science fiction writer's education, and I agree.

Perhaps you have friends of other cultural backgrounds. Talk to them. Explain what you're trying to do. Even though no one is a certified representative of their own ethnic group, they can let you know when something you propose is totally out of whack. And they can point you to sources of specific info.

If you're thinking of approaching someone who's more an acquaintance than a friend, offer to buy them lunch or dinner, and make the interaction a formal interview. This is what you'd do with anyone else you wanted to pump for valuable data. Cultural background is data. If you want it, and you don't have it, it's valuable; treat it that way.

Above all, don't rely on representations of minorities gleaned from popular culture. They're as true to life as Donna Reed's pearl-laden floor-waxing outfits.

So now that you've got some background on these Beautiful Strangers, how best to use it?

A lot depends on your piece's point of view and the size of a given character's role within it. Let's start with Charnas' short story "The Ancient Mind At Work," in which the protagonist, a white immigrant from South Africa, views an African American man:

> Katje never called him by his name because she didn't know whether he was Jackson Somebody or Somebody Jackson, and she had learned to be careful in everything to do with blacks in this country. (16)

> He was slender as a Kikuyu youth—she could see his ribs arch under his shirt.... By rights he belonged in a red blanket, skin gleaming with oil, hair plaited. Instead he wore the tan shirt, pants, and zip-up jacket of an "engineer" from Buildings and Grounds, and his hair was a modest Afro, as they called it, around his narrow face. (19)

Here we see the minority through the eyes of another minority, but one sharing many assumptions with this society's rulers. Katje's opinions about what this man "should" be wearing and doing throw our own preconceptions in relief by their extremity. Her caution in dealing with Jackson underscores that of most American whites.

On a few occasions, Charnas has Jackson speak for himself:

> "Try and don't put nobody in that number-six bedroom till I get to it the end of the week," he said. (19)

> "I got accepted to Computer school in Rochester next semester...they don't do blacks with guns...." (50)

Jackson's speech reflects patterns familiar to anyone who's ever listened to or talked with blacks of a certain upbringing. But it doesn't lapse into incomprehensible "Buckwheatisms"; it marks difference, not inferiority. The combination of honest, foreign prejudice, familiar tension, and Jackson's voicing of his own concerns produces a picture in slightly more than two dimensions, all that's necessary for a supporting character.

Sterling's "Green Days In Brunei" features a multi-transracial cast; main and most supporting roles are filled by people of very different races than the author's own. On assignment for a Japanese corporation, Turner Choi, a twenty-six-year-old Chinese Canadian CAD CAM engineer, becomes slowly accustomed to the ways of a tiny, somnolent country near Borneo, and its mix of Malaysian, Chinese, Iban, Dayak, and European citizenry. Novella length gives Sterling room to flesh Choi out, using comparisons to his stay-at-home, lawyer brother and his domineering, bad-cop, drug tycoon of a grandfather. A non-Asian girlfriend calls him "about as Chinese as maple syrup…" (122) A Malaysian princess sees his status as a Western techie as exotic.

Choi's observations of his surroundings reveal as much about himself as they do about Brunei. The gossipy, village-like *kampongs,* which run the city's retro-greened high-rises, inhibit his bachelor lifestyle. The Dayaks are *his* exotics, the "dark, beautiful descendants of headhunting pirates, dressed in hand-dyed sarongs and ancient plastic baseball caps," (129) their language "utterly incomprehensible." (129)

Otherness is not a uniform state. Non-whites are not identical, interchangeable units. Choi's sense of himself as a foreigner, as a Westerner, a Northerner, and a child of privilege, complicates all his interactions. Age, more than race, distances him from the white exile Brooke, with whom he might otherwise form an alliance.

It's mostly Choi's gear-headedness that defines him for himself. He learns the obsolete programming language required for his assignment so well he dreams in it. And he sees his love for Princess Seria as defined by tech: "The painfully simple local Net filtered human relations down to a single channel of printed words, leaving only a high-flown, Platonic essence. Their relationship had grown into a classic, bloodless, spiritual romance…" (126)

Being a gear-head in low-and-appropriate tech Brunei causes Choi's most alienated moments and allows Sterling his closest identification with the character.

Katmer Al Shei, a heroine of the novel *Fool's War,* shares several characteristics with her creator Sarah

Zettel. They're both women of low stature and high determination. Both rely on discipline and humor to help them deal with trying situations.

For Al Shei, this includes an encounter with a "gerbil," i.e., space-station worker, who assaults her near the book's beginning:

> "Oh, sorry," said a man's bland voice. "I didn't see a *person* there. I thought it was just a pile of rags and shit."
>
> Al Shei pulled herself upright and turned around slowly to face the chestnut- skinned, auburn-haired, totally unshaven can-gerbil.
>
> She drew herself up to her full height. "There is no god but Allah and Muhammad is the Prophet of Allah." Reciting the first pillar of Islam loudly was her standard tactic. Bigots seldom know how to reply to a declaration of faith... (18)

Long before this early and explicit confrontation, Zettel establishes Al Shei's otherness, with descriptions of the veils she and her cousin wear and their integration of prayer into starship routine.

She also gives us a good idea of the context of this otherness. Coloring is noted: Master Fool Evelyn Dobbs' skin is "a clear brown, two or three shades lighter than Al Shei's earth tones. That and the angles in her eyes and her face said a good chunk of her ancestry was European." (5) And "shockingly blue eyes" shine out of Al Shei's brother-in-law Tully's "medium brown face." (16) But the roots of this society's major prejudices lie in a dislike of certain strongly held beliefs. And right down there with the Muslims in terms of popularity is a group called "Freers."

Freers have revolutionary ideas concerning A.I.s and their occasional emergence into self-awareness.

Since these chaotic births usually result in the loss of human life, most people think Freers are insane to encourage them.

Fool's War's narrative viewpoint switches between Al Shei, a target of religious persecution, Freer Jemina Yerusha, and Evelyn Dobbs, who has her own reasons for fearing irrational hatred. Though they all experience prejudice, the heroines' goals aren't quite congruent. Again, varying view points and sources of otherness give the story verisimilitude.

One more note on *Fool's War*: Zettel makes a conscious effort to avoid equating non-European skin tones with food. In fact, she does the opposite, writing of Com Engineer Lipinski's "pale, exotic good looks" in terms of milk and lobsters, which she contrasts with the more customary copper, bark brown, chestnut, etc. A friend pointed out to her the annoying frequency of references to coffee and chocolate as racial color analogies. Humans have been treated as commodities in this hemisphere's recent past. The connection to slavery was subtle, but disturbing, and Zettel has done what she can to reverse the trend.

So let's review how you, too, can make your universe an equal opportunity employer.

First, get to know your subjects. Primary sources are best.

When telling your story from any character's viewpoint, be true to their take on the situation. Don't give them your own anachronistic beliefs or inauthentic, "p.c." motivations.

Allow minority characters to speak with their own voices, even if only in a brief comment. Contrasts between multiple viewpoints produce both diversity and depth.

Show how race and prejudice figure in your setting and what, if any, their connections.

Remember that difference is in the eye of the beholder. Black people don't spend their whole lives thinking of themselves as black. We're Ghanaians and editors and diabetics, and lots of other -ians and -ors and -ics. Use these self-categorizations to add points of audience identification to your characters.

Finally, offer your work to members of other ethnic groups for critique. You don't have to follow their suggestions, but it won't hurt to hear them.

Tom Wolfe spoke at a National Press Club lunch on the subject of "writing what you know." (November 16, 1998, National Press Club, Washington, DC). His point was that this is great advice, but that as writers it's our job to continually know more.

This is true for sf writers in spades cubed. If we can't create a reasonable facsimile of the local cigar shop's owner, how much of a chance do we have of convincing readers they understand the Ganymedian group mind's ambassador?

So welcome the Beautiful Strangers. Don't be afraid to make mistakes with them. Do your best, and you'll avoid the biggest mistake of all: exclusion.

Works Cited

Charnas, Suzie McKee . "The Ancient Mind At Work." *The Vampire Tapestry*. Albuquerque, NM, Living Batch Press, 1980.

Douglass, Frederick. *Narrative of the Life of Frederick Douglass, An American Slave: Written by Himself.* New Haven, CT, Yale University Press, 2001.

Sterling, Bruce. "Green Days in Brunei." *Crystal Express.* Sauk City, WI, Arkham House, 1989.

Stowe, Harriet Beecher. *Uncle Tom's Cabin.* New York, NY, Bantam Classics, 1983.

Zettel, Sarah. *Fool's War.* New York, NY, Warner Books, 1997.

Appropriate Cultural Appropriation

by Nisi Shawl

For some of us, the attractions of another's culture can hardly be overrated. Within the context of speculative fiction's reputation as "escapist" literature, getting away from one's own traditions and background may seem like a good idea. Surely to find that much-prized "sensawunda" sought by genre aficionados we must leave behind what British fantasist Lord Dunsany called "the fields we know?"

But what if the realms beyond these fields are populated? One person's terra incognita is another's home. What are we to make of the denizens of these exotic lands? And what will they make of us, tramping through their yam patches in search of the ineffable, and frightening their flocks with our exclamations over their chimeric beauty?

To collapse the metaphor, readers looking for something "different" in fantastic fiction, and authors who attempt to supply them with it, often turn to mythologies, religions, and philosophies outside the dominant Western paradigm. Then, not too surprisingly, people who practice these religions or espouse these philosophies or descend from those who constructed these mythologies object. Their culture, they complain, is being misrepresented, defaced, devalued, messed with. Stolen. Often said culture is the only resource remaining after colonialization has removed all precious metals from the ground, or the ground from under its former inhabitants feet, or, as in the case of the African slave trade, when it has assumed ownership of those feet themselves.

Hiromi Goto's poem "Notes for an Appropriation Panel" (written during WisCon 27) voices her uneasiness in the face of another author's culture-mining:

#1

my subject positioning does not reflect
your object placement your anthropological
imperative soothed by your liberal heart
we will agree to disagree is your buddhist mantra
as you keep stuffing geisha
into my house

#2

I'm frightened
your imagination is not my reality
I do not trust you
I have read from your imagination for five centuries
I am still starving
you want to think you're doing me a favour
I will bite the hand that feeds me

#3

you are so interested
your eyes are glowing
it's simply fascinating
a tightening in your groin
you want to share it
you've done your research and you got permission
from your native informant
you want me to thank you
you think we will be friends

#4

your inscription has maimed me
a small cut you choose not to see
scars criss cross my body
you turn away from my disfigurement
my critique falls upon your mantra
you would rather gaze upon
your own creation

#5

she is a work of art
almost everyone loves her
you love her
you tug the kimono off her dainty shoulders
her perfectly formed arms
you burrow into her body
the small noises you make are disturbing
in her silence her eyes are open
but she cannot see

#6

I did not want to watch you do this
a lot of people are clapping
you stand up to take a bow
as I leave the auditorium
your creation falls to dust
you do not care you will make another
the only limits are your imagination

Yet if they ignore non-dominant cosmologies and traditions and exclude them from their work and their libraries, writers and readers could be said to have contributed to their erasure. How to resolve this conflict?

Thoughtfully.

To begin with, we can reframe it. Rather than looking at a binary choice between (mis)appropriating a culture and avoiding its mention, we can consider a spectrum of roles its possible for transcultural writers and readers to play.

We can examine works in which authors have attempted to write about or extrapolate from another's culture for ways in which they succeed or fail.

We can question and reground our desire to write about other cultures.

In this essay, I'll do all of the above, to varying and (I hope) entertaining degrees.

During the same panel that inspired Goto's poem, audience member Diantha Day Sprouse categorized those who borrow others' cultural tropes as "Invaders," "Tourists," and "Guests." Invaders arrive without warning, take whatever they want for use in whatever way they see fit. They destroy without thinking anything that appears to them to be valueless. They stay as long as they like, leave at their own convenience. Theirs is a position of entitlement without allegiance.

Tourists are expected. They're generally a nuisance, but at least they pay their way. They can be accommodated. Tourists may be ignorant, but they can be intelligent as well, and are therefore educable.

Guests are invited. Their relationships with their hosts can become long-term commitments and are often reciprocal. (Sprouse, personal communication.)

A good deal of transcultural writing's bad reputation is owing to authors and audiences who act like Invaders. In one unpublished story I've seen, the writer took a sacred song here, a tattoo there, snapped up a feast featuring roasted pig and manioc root from somewhere else and presto! South Pacific Island culture at our fingertips! That this Island's analogue was inhabited by blond, blue-eyed people may have been meant to soften the act of appropriation by distancing readers from its victims. Or the point may have been to allow the blond, blue-eyed author or reader easier identification and access. The effect, unfortunately, was one of cultural theft squared. Not only were the appurtenances of the culture removed from their native settings, they were placed in the hands of people deliberately marked as racially distinct from their originators.

Further controversy is generated when certain authors reject the equivalent of Tourist status, under whatever name that status is presented to them. They prefer to see themselves as Guests: welcome everywhere they go, almost indistinguishable from those born to the cultural territory they're visiting. A territory where they're enjoying themselves so much they keep putting off their scheduled departure.

A Tourist can become a Guest, if the locals like what they see and ask her to return. But before taking on the Tourist role, a writer or reader will have no contact with said locals. When first learning about and incorporating aspects of another's culture, then, we ought to act like the best of all possible Tourists: to stay alert and observant, to watch for the ways our own background influences how we interpret our surroundings. We ought to remember that we have baggage. We ought to be prepared to pay for what we receive (but more about that below). We ought to be honest about the fact that we're outsiders. And since we're in an unfamiliar setting we shouldn't be ashamed of occasionally feeling lost. We ought to swallow our pride at such times and ask for help, ask for directions.

Whom should we ask?

When it comes to non-dominant cultures, there are no officially elected gatekeepers. Particular organizations have heads, councils, spokespersons, and so on, but there's no over-arching authority, no one clearing-house to vet and approve all a writer's transcultural efforts or a reader's interpretation of those efforts.

So while it's best to ask for help, it's unrealistic for an author to expect to be awarded an embossed, beribboned certificate proclaiming the authenticity of her work. All transcultural writers can hope for is understanding and acceptance by readers in general and by individual members of the culture they're attempting to represent in particular.

The bibliography at the end of this essay contains a few suggestions for further reading, among them examples of successful transcultural writing. As to specific techniques I'd recommend for those who want to write this sort of thing, there's some overlap with the previous essay "Beautiful Strangers: Transracial Writing for the Sincere," (75) wherein I enumerate ways to create believable characters of a race other than the author's.

However, members of the same race can frequently come from different cultures, as any North American black who travels in Africa can attest. To a certain extent, members of different races can come from the same culture as well. Culture is both more real and robust than race (a classification once supposed to be biological in nature and now revealed as a social construct), and more ephemeral and fragile: accusations of cultural theft are far more common than accusations of the appropriation of another's race. The sets overlap but aren't identical.

When at all plausible, the best point of view from which to recount a transcultural tale is one that in some way mimics the tale-teller's position vis-à-vis the culture: that of an alien. The correspondence need not be exact. The pov character need not be the author somehow transported to the story's setting. Such a character's distancing can come from other factors. Perhaps they've been raised by someone reluctant or unable to share cultural knowledge, as in Due's *The Good House*. Perhaps they're a member of a racial minority within a non-Western culture, who yet identifies with that culture, as does Chung Mae, ethnic Chinese heroine of Geoff Ryman's *Air*, which is set in the mountains of Karzistan. Or they may have been isolated by a disaster or the act of a colonizing power. And of course, the narrator or pov need not be the story's protagonist.

(A caveat: having a character merely incorporate the author's reaction to that character's own culture will not give you the sort of perspective I'm talking about here. In fact, it will almost always detract from the story's verisimilitude.)

Two recent novels explore how African traditions underpin that most European of myths, the search for the Holy Grail. In *Coyote Kings of the Space-Age Bachelor Pad*, new Canadian writer Minister Faust uses the point of view of the descendants of East African immigrants, divided by centuries and continents from the relevant legacy: the wisdom of Osiris. Alex Irvine, a white writer from the US, gives us multiple narrators in *One King, One Soldier*. All these are also white, but one is possessed by the spirit of a black man, so that while he cannot speak with this man's voice it haunts and inhabits him as he journeys on foot up the Congo.

Additionally, portraying a culture calls for paying attention to setting, dialogue, action, and a host of other elements above and beyond character. While I won't go into these to the same extent that I've looked at character, I can offer some helpful questions:

Is your adopted milieu a "frozen culture"—one that looks like a picture postcard from an exotic locale, hermetically sealed off from developing technologies, the influences of other cultures, even climatic and geological forces? In a way, these settings are just further instances of the same bad writing that fills bookstore shelves with fantasies set in never-ending Middle Ages, but they can exert regrettable influence on how we view current non-Western cultures and their members.

In an effort to create an original setting, have you adopted a "mix-and-match" approach, including some cultural elements while leaving others on the cutting room floor as irrelevant or distasteful? Be aware that material you reject may seem crucial to members or descendants of that culture and may render what you retain inexplicable to them—and to other readers.

Is the culture you're portraying intrinsic to the story, or is it only there to fancy up your depiction of events that might have taken place anywhere, at anytime? Just as some transracial characters come across as no more than color-tinted versions of the author's racial identity, some transcultural settings seem to be no more than the author's home ground with a few representative foreign props scattered around. Science fiction and fantasy stories in which things of a speculative or fantastic nature are tangential to what happens are usually unsatisfying, and an analogy can be drawn from this to the appearance of cultural details in transcultural stories.

Does the characters' dialogue appear as dialect? Actually, all speech is (arguably) in one or another dialect; in attempting accurate transcription of any particular version of English we mark it as nonstandard and in some sense deprivilege it. At the same time, the rhythms and accents of Caribbean speech, for example, are distinctive, and to ignore them would do verisimilitude a disservice. Again, monochromatic or static representation is less likely to ring true. Variations within a culture of characters' vocabularies, inflections, etc., exist, and should be shown. When dealing with characters speaking another language than the one in which the story's written, the choices become more clear-cut, because they're more obviously voluntary. By assigning unusual speech patterns to the adopted culture, a writer will distance her readers from the people of that culture.

Desire, the last item on my outline for this essay, is where it all begins. My introduction mentions the draw of exoticism. Of course motivations are never simple, and a love of the "exotic" can be the product of complex forces. Sometimes a person feels an inner resonance with another culture. My younger sister Julie, for instance, was fascinated as a child with Jewish things—not the religion per se but the culture as a whole: food, music, and so on. Looking back, it seems likely that this was because of the ambiguous status of Jewishness; it's seen as separate in many important ways from dominant white culture, yet was nowhere near as stigmatized as our identity as "Negroes" in the place and time in which we grew up.

In addition, a writer may have other reasons for wanting to write transculturally: to speak for those unheard at one or another level of discourse; to point out similarities between themselves and people generally classified as dissimilar; to hitch a ride on some literary bandwagon such as magical realism; to learn about, understand, and sympathize with members of another culture. Readers have their own versions of most of these motives. Some of these motives are suspect; some are laudable. Some are both.

Many of my ideas on working artistically with another's culture derive from my religion: specifically, from Ifa priest Luisah Teish's thoughts on ancestor worship. In her classic *Jambalaya: The Natural Woman's Book of Personal Charms and Practical Rituals*, she advocates broadening the concept of descent to include the enjoyment of all the benefits we derive from all the world's cultures: "Is your dress made of Japanese silk? Yes? Then revere those ancestors. Having cornbread with dinner tonight? Recognize the work of the Native Americans." (71)

In the same vein, a young character in Samuel R. Delany's short autobiographical novel "Atlantis: Model 1924" declares his intention to originate from everywhere:

> From now on, I come from all times before me—and all my origins will feed me. Some in Africa I get through my daddy.... Some in Europe I get through the library: Greece and Rome, China and India—I suck my origins in through my feet from the paths beneath them that tie me to the land, from my hands opened high in celebration of the air, from my eyes lifted among the stars— (114)

However, any connections I make with unfamiliar cultures must be more than one-way. When acknowledging benefits derived from a cultural source I also acknowledge that I have responsibilities to that source: the responsibility to recognize it, to learn from it, to protect it, to serve it, to enhance it somehow if I can, to promote it to others. The extent to which I do this depends partly on the extent to which I benefit, and partly on the extent to which I'm able to reciprocate that benefit.

Immaterial things—ideas, beliefs, customs, paradigms, and other non-physical artifacts—have value. This is a concept any patent lawyer would agree with; it's something that writers who hope to sell their work are literally banking on. But when applied to the topic of cultural appropriation it elicits protests against "commodification." Culture, though, is commodified daily. The main variables in its commodification are the buyer and the seller. There's no reason I know of that only corporations ought to profit from manipulating this equation. The irony-laden efforts of an eBay entrepreneur to sell his "blackness" online a couple of years ago effectively dramatized commodification's current one-sidedness.

Value fluctuates. If cultural knowledge is information, it can become less valuable when its transmission is masked, like a radio signal, by a lot of noise. The valid information becomes indistinguishable from errors, misinterpretations, and deliberate fabrications made on the part of the transmitter. For instance, I incorporated some elements of Ifa, my religion, in a story of mine called "Wallamelon." But I also imagined a non-existent form of divination as a tradition of the heroine's lineage. I'm arguably devaluing my own (adopted) culture, because of my inclusion of this imaginary rite. However, a non-practitioner will be able to distinguish between actual Ifa and my fabrications by reading the disclaimer I've included on the subject. Honesty and precision are one sort of currency.

Money is another. Some cultures have lots of it; some have less. If you're borrowing creative elements from a non-dominant and/or non-Western culture, consider making a cash donation to some institution that supports, preserves, or furthers the knowledge of that culture.

I'll close with a quote of encouragement for readers and writers in this area from Ryman: "I think that it's a good thing for the imagination to do to try to imagine someone else's life. I see no other way to be moral, apart from anything else. Otherwise you end up sympathising only with yourself. . . ." (Ryman, personal communication.)

Works Cited/Recommended Reading

Cutter, Leah. *Paper Mage*. New York, NY, Roc, 2003.

Delany, Samuel R. "Atlantis: Model 1924." *Atlantis: Three Tales*, Hanover, NH, Wesleyan University, 1995, 113 - 115.

Due, Tananarive. *The Good House*. New York, NY, Atria, 2003.

Faust, Minister. *Coyote Kings of the Space-Age Bachelor Pad*. New York, NY, Del Rey, 2004.

Frost, Gregory. "The Prowl." Hopkinson, Nalo, ed., *Mojo: Conjure Stories*. New York, NY, Warner, 2003.

Irvine, Alexander C. *One King, One Soldier*. New York, NY, Del Rey, 2004.

Jones, Gwyneth. *Divine Endurance*. New York, NY, Arbor House, 1987.

McHugh, Maureen F. *China Mountain Zhang*. New York, NY, Tor, 1992.

Murphy, Pat. *The Falling Woman*. New York, NY, Tor, 1986.

———. *Wild Angel*. New York, NY, Tor, 2000.

Ryman, Geoff. *Air*.

———. *The King's Last Song, or Kraing Meas*. (Forthcoming).

Sellman, Tamara Kaye. "Practical Magic: Understanding the Other." *MARGIN Magazine*, Summer 2004, <http://www.angelfire.com/wa2/margin/pracmagicS04.html>.

Shawl, Nisi. "Transracial Writing for the Sincere." Speculations.com, October 1999, <http://www.speculations.com/transrace.htm>.

———. "Wallamelon." Aeon Magazine, May 2005, <www.aeonmagazine.com>.

Sterling, Bruce. "Maneki Neko." *The Magazine of Fantasy & Science Fiction*, May 1998. *A Good Old-Fashioned Future*, New York, NY, Bantam, 1999.

Teish, Luisah. *Jambalaya: The Natural Woman's Book of Personal Charms and Practical Rituals.* New York, NY, Harper & Row, 1985, 70 - 71.

Excerpt from Nisi Shawl's forthcoming novel

The Blazing World

We conclude this book with an example of fiction by one of the co-authors which employs parallax, congruence, and creative classification.

The Blazing World is the story of someone most of us would find truly "other": a clone whose growth has been artificially stunted. The novel takes place about 300 years in our future, in a landscape changed by nano-scaled manufacturing and bioengineering, a political world torn apart by small, nasty conflicts. Clones such as the heroine Mo Kree (aka Ida) are the possessions of rich, protected classes. For ethical reasons (the stunting process is ultimately fatal) an opposition movement called The Treasure Seekers rescues and rehabilitates selected clones. As this excerpt opens, we join Mo Kree and her rescuer Panther (aka Lina) on their journey along the Columbia River toward the island sanctuary of The Treasure Seekers.

All at once I'm waking up, with Panther shaking my shoulder. She goes up to look around. Before I can even use the bucket she is at the top of the ladder, calling me Ida again. Which must mean there are other people around, and we are back to doing our pretend again.

"Yeah, Mom," I yell. "I'll be right there." I hurry up. A smell of smoke bothers my nose, but it's mostly mist I see. There are some fires, up ahead. They form the shapes of small hills that will pass us on our right. We're in a little side stream of the river, narrower across.

As we get closer to the fires, I see all sorts of boats tied up together, floating without going. Two big fires on either side of us show exactly why. A big net of chains is hanging down into the water from some rocks. Not too high, but our barge or any of the other boats can never get through that. A little kid could, maybe, swimming.

By this time we are up where everyone is waiting. The silvery mist is brighter now. I don't know all these kinds of boats I see. Barges, sure. And some look like the Nortons' nice wooden boat, though a few are made of metal. Others seem to be nothing but bunches of logs with ropes around them. Lots of poles stick up from everything. They hang the sails there. Sails are cloths to catch the wind.

We're pretty high up from the water. My mom points to a small shape moving between the boats. It looks like a long leaf. When it stops beside a barge, I see the shadow of a man sticking out of its middle. "That's a baidarka," Mom tells me. "They're great. I'll teach you to use one when we get home." To the island. She doesn't say that.

The people on the barge lean down and wave their hands at the man. He twists his baidarka away and out of my sight.

I go down to bring up some froots and bredstix for our breakfast. When I get back the mists have suddenly turned pink, and the fires have faded out. I chew a square of sweetness and watch the baidarka coming closer. Now I can see how the man paddling it has no shirt on. Under a yellow hat, his hair hangs down thick and black, but not like my mom's. Straighter. His skin has a nice color where it shines with wetness.

He stops at our side. My mom holds out her hands. I put my other froot between my teeth so I can show him mine.

"Hey, that's one weird tongue you stick out at me, yunitsa." I laugh and bite my froot so half of it falls onto the deck. He screeches and acts stupid. "Oh, no, I don't mean for you to spite your face, yunitsa! Oh, I feel so terrible! A woman without a tongue now, even one so strange as yours was, how shameful! How sorrowful! And I to be the cause...your beautiful mother, how ever will she forgive me this my crime?"

My beautiful mother looks mad. Why? He believes our pretend without us even trying. He's funny, too. But all she says is "Okay. Are you going to let us through?"

"You are impatient, hey? You have waited too long since bearing this last child, till almost she could be called a woman in her own right. Yes. How lucky for you I am gate duty here today. Baida, that is me! Astoria's foremost impregnator, at your service." He flips his paddle high into the air and catches it in one hand above his head, without even looking.

"Fine," my mom says. "Pleased to meet you. Perhaps I will avail myself of your offer after I've seen some of the competition." Neither of them says anything for a moment. Water from his paddle starts dripping down on Baida's hat. "After you've *let us in*," my mom adds.

"Yes. Indeed, I hope I do nothing to hinder you." He points with his paddle and I see how the boats in front of us are moving forward. The metal net in the river has started sinking down. "My companions in the winchtower have understood my signal, which is certainly more importance than if you do. For should you get left behind as the others enter, there lies a charming interval of conversation and instruction until another group accumulates for my inspection. And after that, I will be relieved and may accompany you as you tour the Fair's attrac—Wait! You have yet to—Yunitsa, why does your mother behave so strangely? To walk away while I address her seems so rude!"

Mom has started the barge to move again. "My name's not Yunitsa," I tell the man in the baidarka. He paddles to stay next to us. "It's Ida."

"Aha! Ida and Baida! We rhyme! A sign that we are going to become good friends; wait and see!"

I don't know about that. We're probably going to stay here just a short time. On the island, that's where I'll get to make my friends. I bend over to pick up my piece of froot. Baida is still beside us when I stand back up, but further behind.

"Tea!" he shouts up at me. "I invite you and your beautiful mother to partake with me at the Tent of the Green Peacock. This afternoon! Say yes, yunitsa!"

"All right," I yell back. "Maybe. If Mom says so."

He yells something more from too far away to make sense now. He has stopped his paddling, and we are going over the place of the metal net. So I turn away from him to see what's in front.

The river and the other boats ahead have made most of the noise so far, but now here come other sounds: yells, and bells ringing, and a drum beating like I should go closer and hear better. And all the mists are parted now. As we swing around a bend I see the Fair.

From here all the pieces of it form into pretty patterns. Mom comes back beside me. “We’ll look for a place to stop beyond the center,” she says. “Want to help me drive?”

I enjoy standing here just staring at the sights. The thing is, though, the idea of making the barge move is also exciting. So I head below.

We lie on the floor and scooch up to our shoulders beneath the bunk. The brain is open, and glowing with what the barge sees outside. I put my head in next to my mom’s. By tilting around I look under the water, on the right or left, or up at the morning sky. The barge sees stuff differently. Through things I think are solid, for instance. And farther away than I can. And if we were still on the main, big, part of the river, there’d be a line in yellow flowing down below my belly. Instead, it’s in Follow mode, with a yellow dot floating over the center of the raft Mom picked out for it to focus on. If that one stops too soon, I get to choose another.

“Only a couple of other boats are left in front of us,” I say.

“I thought the others would choose the first moorings they came to.” She sounds satisfied about that. A mooring is a place to put a boat when it is on the water but going nowhere. Because it brought you to where you have to be, Mom says.

We sail past the Fair’s center, and soon there’s mostly just the ground again and the things that always grow there. The barge's brain has an arrow pointing up for speed. As the arrow gets shorter I know we must be slowing down. Probably because that's what the raft does, that Mom told the barge to follow. We are turning right, towards a sort of bridge of wood. It looks like a bridge ending out in the middle of the water. I see the raft pull up next to it and stop. The barge hangs around, confused what to do next.

"Okay," Mom says. "Now we're using 'Find.'" So I tell it colder, warmer, hotter, burning hot, on fire, until the barge is exactly where we want to be.

I want to get out right away. My mom thinks we better wait. Why? The others that we moored up with are tying ropes and climbing up the bridge's legs—actually, the pier's. But it would be better if we didn't have to talk to them. We don't need to be noticed.

So instead we clean up ourselves. I tell Mom about Baida's invitation. She laughs. She says he is a Russian, and far away from where they usually live. "I wonder why he's so sure of himself? Bravado, probably." I learn that bravado is a way of pretending to be brave. It sounds like I could use it.

"I told him we'd be there," I say. My mom says nothing back. She braids my hair without talking.

There's still a bunch of cider left from the Nortons. My mom rolls two bottles inside her blanket, longways, and ties the ends of it into a circle to hang on one shoulder. She puts a circle of rope over her other one, and I copy that with the strap of my medicine box.

It's easy to jump down onto the pier from the railing of our barge. And we find a trail in the tall grass on the pier's land side. The sun is high above, headed for noon.

We go twisting around humpy little hills. No wars to worry about, thanks to the Nortons. Insects sing their high songs and hop away from our moving feet. Bushes of yellow flowers rustle softly from the breezes. I take one into my hands and kiss it.

My mom is a ways ahead. I walk quickly to catch up, keeping in time to the beats of drums starting to be loud enough to hear.

A man in a short white dress comes into our sight. He holds his arms out wide for a hug. Panther stops a few steps away from him. "Welcome home, sister," he says. He stops, too, changes his arms to wave around, like it's his whole Fair to show off to us. "Welcome home!"

Mom nods. She just stands there, waiting for this man to move. He looks around her to see me. "Ahh, a little one! Welcome home, my child." Mom reaches back her hand for me to hold. Everyone sure likes me. Nortons, Baida, this guy, too.

I nod at the man, but I can't think of anything to tell him. Thanks? He keeps staring and I sort of shrug my shoulders. Behind him the path splits in two parts. Some other people in white dresses start to come along them, walking our way. Four. More. I have to hug them all? Suddenly this doesn't seem like such a great place.

But my mom is already going around the man. She pulls me with her off the path, smiling. "Welcome to you, too," she says. We pass him and she bends down and I hear her whisper "Run—like we're playing a game." So I shout "Tag! You're it!" and I race by all the surprised people. My box bumps my butt, and my mom laughs and calls after me "Wait! Ida, you silly! Wait for me!" Of course I don't.

At the top of the next hill I turn around a second to see if everything's okay. And to breathe better. The white people are standing where we left them. My mom's coming pretty slow up the hill. I sit down till she comes.

We head down the hill's far side. I notice different plants here. They grow in groups, with bricks between them. It's a garden. I decide and tell Mom. She smiles, but seems too tired to say anything.

We keep walking along the path, much larger now. On our left-hand side are some very light marks, some trails in the grass. Looking along them I see cloths stretching out to make tents. Up to where we're walking comes a boy, first kid I've seen since Roa. I stop and say hi. He smiles and looks at the ground. He walks with us not saying anything. His hair is smashed down flat everywhere but on top of his head. He has bare feet, and arms sticking out too long from his shirt.

How can I get him to talk to me? Before I figure out an answer he turns right off of our way. He steps behind a short fence of sticks and sits down so I can't see him anymore. A man stands up so I can. Then I hear the sound of water pouring, hitting mud.

Is someone peeing? Without a bathroom or a head or even a bucket? I ask Mom is it all right to stop and find out. She shakes her head no. "If they wanted you to see what was going on over there, Ida, they wouldn't have bothered to put up a fence."

The fence keeps getting bigger and keeps going along between us and the garden. Now we come to a really main path. So many people walking one way and the other. We're behind the backs of a short man with a big tan hat and a pair of gloves he puts on.

Towards us come more and more people. A wet, naked woman has her hair wrapped up in pink and piled on top of her head. A man in a mustache so long it's hanging off his face hurries to catch up with her. By the time they pass us their arms are around the waists of each other. Coming next is a person I can't decide whether to call him a boy or a man. Way bigger than I am, way smaller than my mom. His hair is tall, red curls mixed with brown. On his shoulders some yellow fuzzy thing stands balancing. A bird. It has a beak it opens and closes, letting out loud peeps. After this comes a girl on a horse! The horse, not even running, still goes by fast, jingling its bouncing bells. Spots of color on its sides streak along and are gone. The bells and the smell of it last longest. Like hot straw turning into bread.

Up ahead of us the hat and glove man stops. He has come to a gate to the garden. Also a woman holding onto a wooden cart on three wheels is waiting there. She is turned sideways, blocking up our path. We wait for a moment while they get the gate open and go inside.

The fence changes to bigger sticks placed further apart. I see right through them. This place is full of animals. Big brown shaggy things with huge heads. They ought to be able to make a bunch of noise. Only soft snorting comes from their black noses. They have little, dusty hooves, dark horns, skinny, swatting tails.

In the distance I hear plenty of other animal sounds. We keep going, but they never get much nearer. Wild honking and disgusted sounding laughter, and a few other things mixed up so I have no idea what to call them. Next to the big quiet animals is an area of muttering chickens. Are they supposed to be this big, up to my waist? The bird on the boy's shoulder was a baby one.

And then there are more horses. Magnificent! I can tell they're interested in me, the way they lay their heads along the fence. Their eyes ask me if I have a gift for them. I wish we could go back to the barge and get them something. Would they like chees? Bredstix? I turn around to ask if my mom knows.

She's ducking down beside me on the path with her head tucked in between her knees so she can't see me. I tap my finger on her back and she pulls me down, too, without even looking up. "Shh!" she says.

Are we in trouble? I don't see anything scary or wrong anywhere. My mom's untying the blanket. Whispering. I lean close to hear her. "Limp and dry, limp and dry, withered, flapping, hairless dick of a— Here!" She hands me the bottles and makes her blanket be a big scarf over her head. Standing up by putting a hand on my shoulder, she keeps a little bit bent.

"What's—"

"Tell you in a minute!" She shoves me away from the horses and across the path. I try not to bump into the many more people. They crowd around us till we stand in a line. By bending over, Mom makes a little tent of her light brown blanket. Inside, I see her worried face.

"Ida, dear," she says, "I'm sorry, I had to get us away from there."

"Why? What's the matter?"

"I saw someone I know, someone I wasn't expecting to see here." The line pushes us up. "He may have recognized me from another…pretend."

Again we move forward. In front of us somebody asks what is the show. "Riverdreams," a woman says. "Family entertainment. Whatcha got?"

A teachie here? I peek out of our tent. I see a few more people, and then the tall stump of a dead tree with a woman standing behind it. Behind her is a gate in a fence of more dead trees, locked together by their silver branches. "That'll do 'er," says the stump woman, and two of the people in front of us go through the gate. So the line pushes us up again.

I duck back under the blanket. "What are we gonna do now?" I ask my mom.

"Get inside the show. I'll be able to tell if Rahvee follows us in, and if he does, they have to have another way out."

It comes our turn. The stump lady smiles like she likes me. She has fluffy grey hair and extra lines all over her face. She's old! I give her one of our bottles. "Ain't you a caution? Takin' your ma to the show?" I nod yes. "What's in the bottle, little one?"

"Cider."

"Oooh! All righty, then." She gives me back two flat open shells with wavy holes sliced in their centers. "What's your name, little one?"

"Ida," I tell her.

"Well, Ida, enjoy the show." Everyone here is so nice!

On the other side of the dead trees is a slanting down field full of curving steps. Some people are sitting in rows, close to the bottom. And at the very bottom I see this giant drum, big as a room. Back and over it curves an enormous shell, like the ones I hold in my hand.

My mom has been staying in one place with me to look, too, but now she starts down the field, holding onto my hand. She walks real slowly, and winds up with us sitting several rows above everyone else. She snuggles me closer and says "Keep an eye on the entry for me, Ida. He's not here yet, but he might be further back in line."

I turn around on our log sitting place and lean up against my mom's side again. No one has been coming in behind us, so it's okay so far. Then these three people show up in the gateway. I can tell only one of them's a woman. What's Rahvee look like, anyway?

Mom answers my question right as I open my mouth to ask it. "Watch for a short, thin man with hardly any hair on his head and a bright yellow skirt. And a big dot on his forehead."

Not these guys. They have lots of hair and wear shirts and pants. A big smell of smoke comes off of them as they walk by. I hear them talking and sitting down lower in the field.

More people come in after that. None of them are Rahvee. They're all different from what my mom has said. I see so many faces, but I check to be sure each one isn't Rahvee.

A bell rings, loud and sweet, and it clears everyone's words out of the air. After a quiet moment, more words come from all around us, all saying the same thing in different ways:

Sometimes, I dreams I'm crossing the river, again.

Sometimes I dreams...dreams I'm crossing the river, again.

Sometimes...I dreams I'm crossing the river, *again*.

Whisperings and shouts and wonderings out loud, and then a strong voice starts singing:

Wade in the water!
Wade in the water, children!

This song is coming up from someone's toes and knees and belly. And two high voices join together

with it, just as good, and all these others under
that, singing so powerfully to me:
See those soldiers dressed in white?

Soldiers? What kind of war is this music for? I really, really, really want to turn around and see. Is this the show? No one else ought to be coming in by now.

I twist over my shoulder. Down on the drum a small group of people singing stands. And over the field others are walking toward them. And singing, too. And they are really there, this is *not* a teachie. It's a great big pretend! I *have* to see this. I turn all the way from the gate and sit facing them.

Gai gonna trouble the water!

On the drum they have a stone and a blue bench and a wagon with big wooden wheels; a bag, a tall counter, and a long shimmery blue piece of cloth that lies in a circle around their feet and flutters in the wind. They sing some more:

See those soldiers dressed in blue?
Gai gonna trouble the water!
Must be the little ones will see us through;
Gai gonna trouble the water!

Music rolling over the air rushes right into me. I stand up. I can do this too. I'm singing:

Wade in the water!

They're really there, they see me, they *are*, and I know they do. I dance and clap my hands in time and follow them down to the drum.

Wade in the water, children!
Wade in the water!"

I don't even know what it means, but I am one of its parts. As grand and mysterious as trees, and the deep parts of this music are the dark roots, and the high parts are the lacing of branches arching over us to the sky—

—and I remember last time I felt like this, running away into the woods. Being bad. Spoiled. I drop my hands from clapping. I look behind me. This time, my mom's still there.

She reaches out from under her blanket. Moving also in the music, she wraps me up with her and keeps us walking, over to the side from the center of the drum. Other singers slow down the song, dragging it deeper, lower, quieter now. Somehow I know we're going to stop this soon.

Gai gonna trouble the wa-a-a-ter!

And then the song is over. Only humming keeps the tune. The show is on. And we are in it.

Biographies

Nisi Shawl's short stories have been published widely, including in *Asimov's Science Fiction Magazine*; *Strange Horizons*; *Mojo: Conjure Stories*; and the *Dark Matter* anthologies of science fiction by Afro-diasporic writers. Her fiction collection *Filter House*, from Aqueduct, was a Co-winner of the 2008 James Tiptree Jr. Award. Her reviews and essays have appeared regularly in the *Seattle Times* since the turn of the millennium, and she is a contributor to *The Encyclopedia of Themes in Science Fiction and Fantasy* and to *The Internet Review of Science Fiction.* A board member for the Clarion West Writers Workshop, she likes to relax by pretending she lives in other people's houses. She was a Guest of Honor at WisCon 2010.

Cynthia Ward was born in Oklahoma and has lived in Maine, Spain, Germany, Seattle, and the San Francisco Bay Area. She has published stories in *Asimov's SF Magazine*, *Bending the Landscape: Horror*, and other anthologies and magazines, and has written articles and reviews for *Locus Online*, *SF Weekly*, and other magazines and webzines. Her market-news columns appear in *Speculations* (http://www.speculations.com) and *The SFWA Bulletin* (http://www.sfwa.org/bulletin/). Her website is at http://www.cynthiaward.com.